D1263843

WITHDRAWN

THE JOHN HARVARD LIBRARY

MEMOIR OF
JAMES JACKSON

THE ATTENTIVE AND OBEDIENT SCHOLAR,
WHO DIED IN BOSTON,
OCTOBER 31, 1833,
AGED SIX YEARS AND ELEVEN MONTHS

By His Teacher,
MISS SUSAN PAUL

Edited by
LOIS BROWN

HARVARD UNIVERSITY PRESS
CAMBRIDGE, MASSACHUSETTS
LONDON, ENGLAND
2000

Library of Congress Cataloging-in-Publication Data

Paul, Susan, fl. 1837.
 Memoir of James Jackson, the attentive and obedient scholar, who died
in Boston, October 31, 1833, aged six years and eleven months / by his
teacher, Miss Susan Paul ; edited by Lois Brown.
  p. cm. — (The John Harvard library)
 Originally published in 1835.
 Includes bibliographical references.
 ISBN 674-00092-7 (cloth : alk. paper) — ISBN 674-00237-7
(pbk. : alk. paper

 1. Jackson, James, 1826–1833. 2. Afro-American children—
Massachusetts—Boston—Biography. 3. Free Afro-Americans—
Massachusetts—Boston—Biography 4. Boston (Mass.)—Biography.
5. Afro-American children—Education—Massachusetts—Boston—
History—19th century. 6. Afro-American children—Massachusetts—
Boston—Social conditions—19th century. I. Title: Memoir of James
Jackson. II. Brown, Lois, 1966–   . III. Title. IV. Series.

F73.9.N4 P38 2000
974.4′6100496073′0092—dc21
[B]   99-051781

For my parents—

my first and best teachers

Acknowledgments

THIS BOOK was made possible by the generous and enthusiastic support of colleagues and friends. Joan Jacobs Brumberg and Margaret Washington provided me with invaluable and inspirational examples of what it means to write and rewrite history. Their insistence that I publish this edition of Susan Paul's memoir, their encouragement as I wrote, and their scrutiny of drafts helped this volume take shape and take flight. I am deeply grateful for their constancy, interest, and belief. Dorothy Mermin's steady hand has steadied my own. Her attentive, expeditious responses and suggestions helped me to refine this work, to mature as a scholar, and to gain a clearer sense of how best to produce and craft narratives of literary history. For their willingness to step into the world of antebellum Boston and consider the life of Susan Paul, her community, school, and students, to read drafts of this work, and to talk about reading practices, Boston's black community, and African American history and education, I thank Katherine Butler-Jones, Graham Hodges, Barbara Sicherman, and Jill Watts. For his spirited interest in my work, his generous gifts of information and rare materials, and our enlightening, delightful conversations about nineteenth-century New England life, I thank Richard Newman.

The helpful staff at the American Antiquarian Society, the Bienecke Library at Yale University, the Boston Athenaeum, the Boston Public Library, the Rare Books and Manuscripts

Division of the Butler Library at Columbia University, the Olin Library at Cornell University, the Forbes Library of Northampton, Massachusetts, the Rare Books Division of the General Theological Seminary of the Protestant Episcopal Church, The Library Company of Philadelphia, the Massachusetts Historical Society, the Massachusetts State Archives, the National Archives Center in Lenox, Massachusetts, and the Oberlin College Library Special Collections contributed to the production of this volume. I especially thank Julie Copenhagen and the staff of the Olin Library Interlibrary Loan Department at Cornell University for obtaining vital materials with patience and persistence. Additional thanks to Georgia Barnhill, Marie Lamoureux, and Laura Wasowicz of the American Antiquarian Society for their insightful suggestions. Jane Rodgers Siegel of the Rare Books and Manuscripts Division of Columbia University made an exceptional effort to help me solve some unexpected mysteries surrounding the *Memoir*.

Research was funded in part by faculty research grants from Cornell University and Mount Holyoke College.

It has been a pleasure and honor to work with Aïda Donald of Harvard University Press, who made this, my first book, an exceptionally memorable and rewarding experience. I also owe thanks to Gail Graves for all the good news she bestowed upon me, to Elizabeth Suttell and Ann Hawthorne for their generous editorial support and guidance, and to my anonymous readers for their helpful and practical comments.

Additional thanks for their unwavering support and friendship go to Naomi André, Karen-edis Barzman, David Brumberg, Jonathan Culler, Dacia Gentilella, Catherine John, Cynthia King, Robin Lydenberg, Joyce Marsh, Elizabeth Pryor, Peggy Ramirez, Naledi Saul, Elizabeth Savage, Patrice Scott, Eleanor Shattuck, Sara Wolper, the members of my string "court"et—Kathy Cook, Marilyn Kusek, and Suzanne Walsh—and my colleagues at Mount Holyoke College who have welcomed me so warmly to New England.

And finally, a word of heartfelt gratitude to my family—my parents and sister, Anna, who have been steadfast anchors for me, ever confident and loving during this time of writing and revision.

Contents

Illustrations

MEMOIR OF JAMES JACKSON

Introduction

IN 1831 BOSTONIAN and pioneering feminist speaker Maria Stewart issued a call to her African American sisters: "Awake! No longer sleep nor slumber, but distinguish yourselves. Show forth to the world that you are endowed with noble and exalted faculties. O ye daughters of Africa!" she asked pointedly, "what have you done to immortalize your names beyond the grave?"[1]

Four years later, twenty-six-year-old Susan Paul (1809–1841) answered that call by publishing the *Memoir of James Jackson, the attentive and obedient scholar, who died in Boston, October 31, 1833, aged six years and eleven months*. In doing so she became the author of the first African American biography, and the first American to write a work of evangelical juvenilia about a real rather than imagined African American child. The volume with unadorned pasteboard covers was priced at twenty-five cents and was soon displayed alongside works by Phillis Wheatley and Lydia Maria Child in the downtown Boston bookshop of the Massachusetts Anti-Slavery Society, located on Washington Street.

Paul's chronicle of the life of James Jackson Jr. (1827–1833) was based chiefly on her daily experiences as his primary school instructor, Baptist Sunday school teacher, and family friend. Combining eyewitness accounts, personal testimony, and excerpts from traditional Sunday school texts, the *Memoir of James Jackson* is an impressive document of social history rooted in nineteenth-century evangelicalism and the experiences of free African Americans.

Paul's turn to authorship was undoubtedly influenced by her family's pioneering work and political activism. Her father, Thomas, was pastor of the African Church, also known as the Belknap Street Church, a primary institution in Boston's African American community. Her uncles Nathaniel and Benjamin Paul, also Baptist ministers, were at the forefront of the antebellum struggle to abolish slavery and to establish stable, productive African American communities in the United States and Canada.[2] The *Memoir* appears to be a reflection of Susan Paul's political desire to advocate racial equality in the antebellum North. "There is, surely, sufficient in this little book," she wrote, "to convince all who are candid, that the moral and intellectual powers of colored children are inferior to the power of others, only as their advantages are inferior. Let, then, this little book do something towards breaking down that unholy prejudice which exists against color." In the preface to the *Memoir* Susan Paul declared herself an advocate of the African American community's most defenseless members: the "children of our brethren have too long been neglected. There is among them many a gem, and whose is the guilt that they are not brought out from among the rubbish and polished?"

Paul's *Memoir,* all but neglected until now, reshapes our understanding of African American literary traditions.[3] It predates by twenty-one years Josephine Brown's *Biography of an American Bondman* (1856), the life story of her father,

William Wells Brown, previously hailed as the first biography by a black woman, and thus dramatically revises the timeline for African American biography. The *Memoir* also confirms the early and formative influence of women on the genre of African American biography. Paul's assertion of James Jackson's humanity and the exemplary nature of his life provides an invaluable lens through which to reconsider foundational African American texts such as Frederick Douglass' *Narrative of the Life* (1845), the narrative of Sojourner Truth (1850), Harriet Wilson's *Our Nig* (1859), and Harriet Jacobs' *Incidents in the Life of a Slave Girl* (1861). Although both Susan Paul and her subject were freeborn African Americans, in the *Memoir* she addresses primary issues found in early writings by former and fugitive slaves: slavery and freedom, segregation and assimilation, religious awakening and spirituality. Finally, Paul's discussions of African American elementary and Sabbath school education invite attention to education and childhood socialization, rarely studied aspects of nineteenth-century African American life.

IN HER PREFACE to the *Memoir* Paul acknowledges the scarcity of early biographical details in her chronicle of James's intellectual and spiritual development: "The circumstances in which he was placed, the first four years of his life, rendered it impracticable . . . to present as many particulars as might be deemed desirable." Her comment implies a context of domestic upheaval and family difficulties. In Chapter I Paul tells us that James's "parents lived in Boston," that his father,

James Jackson, was "a respectable coloured man," and that
James Jr. was born on December 5, 1826. In 1826 the Jacksons lived on Butolph Street, in the heart of Boston's African
American neighborhood. The 1820 federal census of Massachusetts and Boston city directories for 1820–1823 and 1825–
1826 show that during this period the family moved six times,
but also that such constant domestic upheaval was not un-
common in the African American community. However, the
Jacksons never moved far from the religious and social center of their community, namely, their church. Their resi-
dences on South Russell, Cambridge, Vine, and Butolph
Streets situated the Jacksons squarely in African American
Beacon Hill and close to the African Church and its school,
on Belknap Street. In 1821 both the Jackson and Paul families
lived on Cambridge Street, one of the principal streets in the
black community.[4]

The 1820 census for Massachusetts is the only one containing a definitive entry for the Jackson family. There the
Jacksons are identified as a family of "Free Colored Persons"
living on South Russell Street in Boston's sixth ward. James
Jackson is the head of household; the family consists of a
male and a female between the ages of twenty-six and forty-
five, and three boys under the age of fourteen.[5] Paul's narrative suggests that James had at least two brothers and two
sisters. Paul reports that "before James was two years old, his

Opposite:
Boston's African American neighborhood, 1835

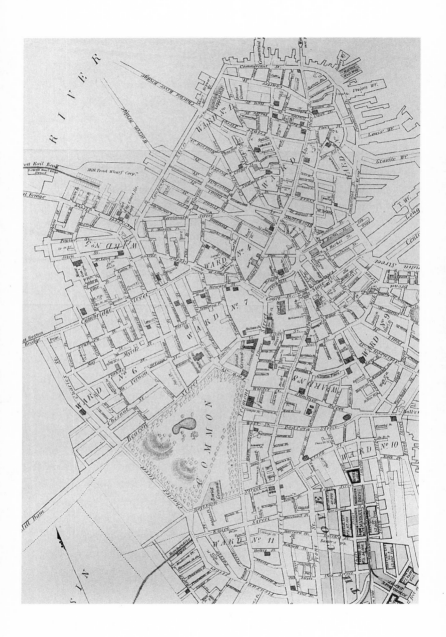

father was taken sick, and after suffering a great deal he died." After the death of James Jackson Sr., probably in 1827 or 1828, his family disappeared from the public record, and their whereabouts during the next ten years are unknown.[6]

The identity of Mrs. Jackson remains an even greater mystery than the family's actual size or later places of residence. Although Paul gives James's mother a powerful role in the *Memoir*, she provides no identifying details such as name, age, or occupation, and the 1830 and 1840 census reports do not identify with certainty a Jackson widow. James's mother may have been named Anna, Fanny, or Hannah; all emerge as possibilities from the city directories and the census.[7]

UNLIKE HER YOUNG STUDENT JAMES, Susan Paul belonged to a well-known and influential New England family whose pioneering work in the ministry and the abolitionist movement has been well documented.[8] Susan was the second of three children born to the Reverend Thomas Paul (1773–1831), minister of the first black Baptist church in the North and Boston's oldest African American church, and his wife, Catherine. By the time of Susan's birth, in 1809, Thomas Paul had been involved in Boston's black religious life for at least twenty years. His earliest recorded participation dates to 1789, when, at the age of sixteen, he performed as "an exhorter of scripture passages" at segregated religious meetings at Faneuil Hall.[9] In 1806, newly ordained as a Baptist minister, Paul was appointed pastor of the African Church

The African Church, ca. 1892

on Belknap Street, a two-story brick building built entirely by African American labor.[10] Paul's initial congregation numbered twenty-four; by 1820 the number had grown fourfold.[11] In 1823 Paul's congregation endorsed his temporary ministry in New York City, where he and a group of disfranchised African American churchgoers founded what became the Abyssinian Baptist Church, later the home church of minister and U.S. Congressman Adam Clayton Powell Jr. When he returned to Boston, Paul resumed his ministry at the African Church, preached extensively throughout New England, and traveled in Haiti for four months as a representative of the Massachusetts Baptist Home Missionary Society. His ill health and tensions within the congregation led to his resignation as pastor in 1829. Paul died of tuberculosis in 1831.

Thomas Paul's career provided his family with relative stability. His prominent ministerial roles and social activism exposed his children to passionate debates about slavery, abolition, colonization, and segregation as well as to evangelical Protestant doctrine. Susan witnessed her father's famous baptisms in Boston Harbor and met influential Americans of both races, including David Walker, author of the incendiary 1829 *Walker's Appeal in Four Articles;* the beloved community leader William Cooper Nell; and the lecturer and essayist Maria Stewart, at whose 1826 marriage Thomas Paul presided.[12] As a young adult Susan worked closely with such outspoken, celebrated, and controversial figures as fellow antislavery society member Lydia Maria Child and William Lloyd Garrison, the fiery abolitionist orator and editor of *The Liberator.*[13]

Thomas and Catherine Paul sought to provide their children with "a good character, and a good education."[14] Susan, Anne Catherine (1807–1835), and Thomas Jr. (1812–1885) may have attended the school housed in their father's church or one of the small private schools that catered specifically to African Americans.[15] Like many middle-class families, the Pauls saw to it that their son received more formal educational training than their daughters. In 1825 at least, thirteen-year-old Thomas Jr. had private tutoring from the Reverend William Bascom, the white instructor at the school housed in the Belknap Street Church.[16] In 1841 Thomas Jr. became the family's first college graduate, receiving a degree from Dartmouth College.[17]

The name Paul was synonymous with African American education and uplift in the early 1800s. When the Belknap Street Church was completed, Thomas Paul and the building committee agreed that the church's basement would serve as a school. Students in the small, independent African American school conducted in the home of the highly respected Primus Hall, a prosperous soapmaker and founder of the first African American Masonic lodge, moved onto the church premises, where the school remained for nineteen years.[18] From 1819 through 1821 the Reverend Paul was an administrative officer for the Boston School Committee. During this time his responsibilities included compiling quarterly reports on African American schools in the city and serving on appointment committees.[19]

Educating Boston's African American youth soon became a Paul family affair. In 1824 Susan's mother, a teacher in her own private school, accepted a city appointment as the head schoolmistress of the public African School Number 2, on Southac Street. The Boston School Committee, usually unenthusiastic about African American educational matters, was surprisingly supportive of Catherine Paul's achievements. One of her first reforms involved moving the school into the family home on George Street. Although the new schoolroom was apparently "not so large as the former," it was "more airy and central," and the committee endorsed the school's relocation on the grounds that there was an "advantage to be derived from its being under the roof of the Rev. Mr. Paul," whose "influence . . . kindly and judiciously exercised both in and out of school, is of great service."[20] The committee's prosegregation motives do not obscure the fact that its members valued Paul's character, respectability, and Christian sensibilities. After several years Susan succeeded her mother, teaching at the school until 1838.[21]

The Paul children benefited from their father's stature as a minister and their mother's undisputed respectability as a teacher. The parents' accomplishments in the two most popular professional occupations among African Americans at this time assured them considerable social, religious, and political influence in the black community.[22] All three children followed their parents' example of social activism and community outreach. Susan and her sister, Anne Catherine, became highly respected primary school and Baptist Sabbath school teachers in Boston, and Thomas Jr. became a well-known teacher and school administrator in Massachusetts, New York, and Rhode Island.[23]

Susan Paul's commitment to abolition and social reform intensified during her early twenties. Fittingly in terms of the later *Memoir,* she began by incorporating African American children into the abolitionist movement. In 1832, one year after her father's death, she formed a Juvenile Choir whose concerts raised funds for the abolitionist movement and needy ethnic groups such as the Mashpee Indians.

The Juvenile Choir was made up entirely of students from Paul's African American primary school, Boston Primary School Number 6. Undaunted by racist policies that prevented her from booking certain venues for the two-hour concerts, Paul located alternative sites. Concerts were advertised prominently in Garrison's *Liberator,* and her future publisher, James Loring, was among the merchants who organized ticket sales from their downtown shops.[24] Performances were frequently sold out, and at least twice the choir met requests from fans for additional concerts. One enthusiastic auditor in 1837 reported that at an early spring performance at Boston's Masonic Temple, the eyes of the fifty children assembled "sparkled with sprightliness, and their countenances beamed with intelligence . . . the sweetness and melody of their voices is incomparable." He added, "Many

JUVENILE CONCERT,

UNDER THE DIRECTION OF

MISS SUSAN PAUL,.

AT COLUMBIAN HALL.

☞ A JUVENILE CONCERT of the Colored Children, constituting the Primary School, No. 6, under the direction of Miss Susan Paul, will be given at COLUMBIAN HALL on TUESDAY EVENING NEXT, February 4, 1834, at 7 o'clock.

ORDER OF EXERCISES.

Overture.—Marseilles Hymn.

PART I.

1. *Duet & Chorus.*—If ever I see.
2. *Chorus.*—In school we learn.
3. *Duet & Chorus.*—The Lark.
4. *Duet & Chorus.*—Ye who in bondage pine.
5. *Duet & Chorus.*—Pleasures of Innocence.
6. *Chorus.*—This, this is our Home.
7. *Solo & Chorus.*—Strike the Cymbal.

Grand Symphony.

PART II.

1. *Chorus.*—O speed thee, speed thee.
2. *Recitative & Chorus.*—Suffer little children to come unto me.
3. *Chorus.*—Little Wanderer's Song.
4. *Chorus.*—The Little Weaver.
5. *Solo & Chorus.*—Prayer for the Commonwealth.
6. *Duet & Chorus.*—Good Night.

☞ Tickets 25 cents each; to be had at the Bookstore of Dea. James Loring, Washington-street; at the store of Mr. James G. Barbadoes, No. 26, Brattle-street; at the office of the Liberator; and at the door of the Hall.   Jan. 4.

Notice of a Juvenile Choir concert conducted by Susan Paul, *The Liberator,* February 1, 1834 of the pieces were difficult; yet they were performed with such correctness and propriety, as to show that not only the teacher, but the children, must have some practical knowledge of the science of music. It could not be all imitation. The pronunciation was distinct, and as correct as will be heard in conversation in any circle of refined society."[25] It is likely that as a student in Paul's primary school, James Jackson participated in these acclaimed concerts. The *Memoir* confirms his familiarity with hymns, and the choir included children as young as age three.

Published programs and reviews of the concerts indicate that Paul and other teachers in the city's African American schools incorporated lessons about slavery into their curriculum. Songs such as "Ye who in bondage pine," "The petition of the sugar making slave," and "Hark to the clank! What means that sound? 'Tis slavery shakes its chain!" had manifest political content. According to a Boston-based contributor to the *New York Evangelist*, a Presbyterian periodical edited by Joshua Leavitt, such songs "produced no small emotion, from their bearing upon a certain 'delicate subject,' coming as they did from those who must *feel* their meaning." The unnamed spectator noted that in some of their songs the children presented "the most pointed and conclusive, as well as touching argument[s]" against controversial political plans such as colonization.[26]

Through her work with the Juvenile Choir, Paul embodied the ideals of antebellum evangelical womanhood, which according to historian Anne Boylan "combined the traditional Protestant ideal of the 'vertuous woman' with a new evangelical stress on action."[27] Paul's philanthropic and antislavery work materialized within her black community, and specifically in her church community, but it probably also received inspiration from women's uplift efforts in cities such as Philadelphia, whose African American communities established mutual-relief and benevolent societies in the late 1790s, and from philanthropic efforts in New York City, where her uncle Benjamin Paul worked closely with groups such as the New York African Mutual Aid Society and the African Dorcas Association in the late 1820s.[28]

Despite her enlightened antebellum home and family tradition of service and outreach, Paul was still to a large degree constrained by nineteenth-century gender roles and expectations. The Paul women's prominence in education and in the abolitionist and African American temperance movements did not receive publicity and detailed documentation. Both African American and white male activists may have more or less consciously collaborated to support such obscurity in the face of increasing female activity outside the home. As historian Harry Reed suggests, the paternal supervision of women's activities, which included such things as booking meeting halls in their names and reprinting minutes of meetings that did not include any detailed list of female members, meant that, like so many other women of the day, Susan Paul and her female colleagues were "protected" by the paternal figures in their worlds.[29]

Susan Paul's transition from private, domestic work to

public, reform activity was probably expedited by family precedents. The ministerial and educational roles of Thomas and Catherine Paul would have helped their daughters gain the approval of church elders and other civic leaders as they began to do increasingly public, interracial, regional, and even national reform work.[30] In 1833, at age twenty-four, she paid fifteen dollars to the New England Anti-Slavery Society and became one of its youngest and first female lifetime members. In the same year she was elected secretary of the Ladies Temperance Society, a new African American organization founded in her Beacon Hill community; within a year the society's hundred members had convinced more than a hundred other African Americans to abstain from liquor and take the "cold water pledge."[31] In 1834 Paul became one of the first African American women to be invited to join the Boston Female Anti-Slavery Society (BFASS), founded the previous year with twelve members. William Lloyd Garrison encouraged the group to integrate its ranks; it did so and not only admitted Susan Paul but immediately appointed her to the position of counselor.[32]

The publication of the *Memoir of James Jackson* in 1835 coincided with tumultuous events in Paul's family circle and in the BFASS. The *Memoir* was first mentioned and excerpted in the June 27, 1835, issue of *The Liberator*.[33] Published alongside the excerpts was a long and moving obituary of her sister, Anne. Anne's death had serious economic as well as emotional effects on the unmarried twenty-six-year-old. The three adult Paul children had lived at 6 George Street with their mother since 1833, but now Susan took on primary responsibility for her sister's four children, ranging in age from a newborn to an eight-year-old. Mourning conventions also dictated a reduction in public activities; in the eighteen months following Anne's death, Susan organized no juvenile concerts, and there is no recorded mention of her participation in other musical or social events.

Paul did not abandon the antislavery cause or her colleagues, however. In late October 1835 she helped to defend her society's mission and its right to convene. The summer of 1835 was, according to *Liberator* editor William Lloyd Garrison, a "reign of terror" in response to increasingly vigorous antislavery campaigns. In October the BFASS invited Garrison's friend, the outspoken British abolitionist George Thompson, to speak at its annual meeting. Word of Thompson's impending appearance led an angry mob to gather outside the BFASS headquarters on Washington Street. In light of the threats against Thompson and the society's inability to book a meeting place because of proprietors' fears about property damage, the BFASS rescheduled the meeting and advertised William Lloyd Garrison as the alternate speaker; but because notices about the meeting did not clarify whether Thompson had in fact been replaced, tensions in the city remained high. When Garrison arrived at BFASS headquarters for the meeting, he found Susan Paul there with Mary Parker, Henrietta Sargent, three Chapman sisters, and some twenty-five other members. Soon the enormous, increasingly belligerent crowd threatened to overrun the building. Paul and her colleagues, having voted to relocate the meeting, were escorted out of the building by Boston mayor Theodore Lyman and police constables. The women walked arm in arm through the raucous mob to the relative safety of Maria Chapman's downtown home. According to Garrison biographer Henry Mayer, "Hisses, sarcastic cheers, and racial epithets assailed the procession, which gradually doubled in size as some of the [BFASS] members detained in the crowd broke free to join their sisters on the march to Mrs. Chapman's house, just off the Common on West Street, seven blocks south." Unbeknownst to Paul and the other women, Garrison remained in the building. Moments after the women left he tried to escape through a window but was soon captured and nearly lynched.[34]

Her sister's untimely death and the escalation of hostilities toward African Americans and antislavery workers may have reinforced Susan Paul's personal and political convictions. From 1835 through 1840 her antislavery and social reform activity increased. In 1837 she was one of four BFASS delegates to the annual Women's Anti-Slavery Convention in New York City.[35] At the next year's convention she was elected one of the conference's vice presidents.[36] In 1840 she joined Lydia Maria Child, Henrietta Sargent, and Anne and Deborah Weston as a BFASS delegate to the annual meeting of the American Anti-Slavery Society. The publication of her *Memoir* undoubtedly played a role in Paul's increasing prominence. Her membership in an elite group of published women of color, her facility with language, and her demonstrated ability to analyze complex social and racial issues made her a valuable asset to the abolitionist and temperance movements.[37]

During these years, however, Paul was increasingly overwhelmed by domestic responsibilities, poverty, and ill health. By 1837, as she began to take on leadership roles in the BFASS and the community at large, she was essentially the head of a household, responsible for providing for her widowed mother, her younger brother, and her dead sister's four children. Family expenses began to mount, and although she supplemented her teacher's salary by taking in sewing, overwork, poor housing conditions, illness, and stress began to take an irrevocable toll. Whatever prospect of support—emotional, financial, or political—marriage might have brought her vanished when her fiancé died of tuberculosis in 1840.[38] Throughout these years, however, Paul maintained her commitments to the BFASS, helping to organize fundraising fairs and representing the organization at national conventions. Weakened by her responsibilities, she eventually contracted tuberculosis.[39] She was finally overcome by the disease during a BFASS fundraising rally in December 1840: "Though at that time in slender health, she presided at one of the tables at the Fair . . . from which she was removed to a sick chamber and the bed of death."[40] Four months later, at the age of thirty-two, she died of consumption.

Susan Paul was mourned by friends, family, and colleagues as a "clear sighted and steady friend," a woman whose "life of severe duty" was "crowned by a triumphant

Died,

In this city, on Monday morning last, Miss SUSAN PAUL, aged about 32, daughter of the late Rev. Thomas Paul. Miss Paul was, for a number of years, a teacher in one of the primary schools of the city—composed exclusively of colored children; and she discharged the duties of her situation in the most satisfactory manner. Being among those, who, in this country, are crushed to the earth on account of the complexion which it has pleased the Creator to give them, she felt and ever manifested a deep and lively interest in the anti-slavery enterprise, and was long an esteemed and useful member of the Boston Female A. S. Society. Though at that time in slender health, she presided at one of the tables at the Fair held by the Society in December last; from which she was removed to a sick chamber and the bed of death. Her disease was consumption. She had acquired an excellent education; her talents and address were of a high order; and she was in all respects qualified to adorn the best circle of human society. Her lot, since she arrived at womanhood, has been a very severe one—marked all along by sorrow, disappointment, adversity; yet it was met with an indomitable spirit and extraordinary fortitude. She has had to provide for an aged mother, and also for four children of a deceased sister, who are now left in a state of utter destitution, and whose condition should excite the commiseration and call into exercise the generosity of the friends of suffering humanity. May the God of the widow and the fatherless raise them up friends and benefactors! We shall be most happy to receive in their behalf, and to appropriate to their relief, any donations that sympathizing friends may wish to contribute for that object. As the Rev. Mr. Paul was a distinguished and highly esteemed Baptist preacher, we trust that a *denominational* interest will be taken in their case; and, especially, that every Baptist clergyman in this city will do something to relieve their pressing necessities.

It is only about a year since Miss Paul followed to the grave, one to whom she had pledged the best affections of her heart, and to whom she had fondly expected to be speedily united in the bands of wedlock. They had anticipated much of earthly bliss; but it has pleased the Almighty to consign them both to an early grave. It is confidently believed, however, that their spirits are now united in heavenly bliss; for, being reconciled to God, through his beloved Son, death had for them no terrors—the grave no gloom. 'Blessed are the dead who die in the Lord.'

The funeral services will take place in the Belknap street meeting-house, on Sunday next, at the close of the afternoon services.

Obituary of Susan Paul, *The Liberator,* April 23, 1841

death in Christ."[41] Charles Ray, editor of the New York–based *Colored American*, reprinted Paul's obituary in *The Liberator* with a preface in which he sympathized with her "deeply afflicted mother and brother, at the loss of so excellent and worthy a daughter and sister." He continued, "The community, as well as the family, have indeed sustained a loss which will not easily be made up."[42] Benjamin Bacon, secretary of the New England Anti-Slavery Society, wrote an unabashedly passionate eulogy of his young colleague. "My heart is sad when I think of the loss which our cause sustains in the death of SUSAN PAUL," he declared in the May 28, 1841, *Liberator*. "Many are abolitionists from the mere force of circumstances," said Bacon. "Not so with Miss Paul. The simple fact that oppression existed was enough to call forth her most self-denying efforts for its overthrow. Nothing but the willful perversion of her mental constitution could have made her otherwise than the uncompromising enemy to slavery in every form. Peace to her memory!" Susan Paul's *Memoir of James Jackson* stands as a tribute not only to the remarkable child she knew but also to the political and racial commitments she embodied in her own short, exemplary life.

THE *MEMOIR OF JAMES JACKSON* was published in Boston just months after the March opening of the Smith School, an expansive new structure in Smith Court that cost nearly eight thousand dollars, was reportedly able to accommodate nearly two hundred students, and made it possible to relocate students permanently from the increasingly uninhabitable basement classrooms in the Belknap Street African Church.[43] Despite the city's apparent investment in African American education, it was clear that segregated education, even in a brand-new structure like the Smith School, was no guarantee of equal opportunity in education or society. By the mid-1830s African American freedom, literacy, education, and social advancement were increasingly controversial issues in the North and South. Federal, state, and community campaigns to monitor, restrict, or abolish African American education gained momentum in the years following the Nat Turner revolt of 1831, an event that was often held up as an example of how knowledge and informed spirituality not only made slaves unfit for servitude, but promoted general civil unrest and threatened social order.

In the *Memoir of James Jackson* Susan Paul provided a record of antebellum African American education, promoted its constructive results, and challenged the myth that the race's enlightenment threatened society and the nation. The subtitle alone, referring to James Jackson as "the attentive and obedient scholar," challenged the reasoning behind African Americans' educational disfranchisement.

In the late eighteenth and early nineteenth centuries, African Americans were legally allowed to attend any of Boston's schools but were often disheartened by the racism they faced there. Once schools for African Americans were established in their own community, students flocked to learn in these more supportive environments. The first city-supervised segregated school, established in 1806 in the basement of the African Church, quickly became overcrowded. A second primary school, also located on Belknap Street, opened shortly thereafter. In the early 1820s a third school for African Americans was organized in Boston's North End.[44] The establishment of additional schools in the 1820s seemed to indicate that a new era in African American education had begun.[45]

But despite great efforts to fund and hire teachers in these separate institutions, historians suggest that most of the city's black school-age children were not in school. Some scholars propose that low attendance in this period was due in part to the economic pressures facing black families and to the inconvenient locations of the schools for some.[46] The all-white Boston School Committee, on the other hand, proposed that attendance was low because African American parents had to be "convince[d] of the importance of education to their children."[47] Susan Paul used the *Memoir of James Jackson* to counter charges that African Americans were neither interested in education nor able to educate themselves in the segregated schools.

Given her own and her family's roles in the segregated African American schools, Paul was undoubtedly aware of the prevailing stereotypes about African Americans and the everyday challenges that black parents and their children faced inside and outside of school. She must also have been mindful of the potential for violence both against women

who advocated equal educational rights and against the black
students they enrolled. In 1833, just months before the death
of James Jackson, there was a violent community attack on a
white teacher, Prudence Crandall, and her newly established
African American female academy in Canterbury, Connecticut. As James and Lois Horton note in their discussion of the
Crandall case, in such educational endeavors children often
bore the brunt of community outrage.[48] The harassment of
Crandall, the attacks on her school, and the endangerment of
her young African American students may have influenced
Paul's decision about how best to negotiate the volatile debate about African American education. She avoided explicit
statements about school segregation and focused instead on
the African American classroom as an enabling and productive sphere. She presented proof of black students' capacity
for formidable intellectual advancement in an environment in
which school, church, and home as American institutions
were united in their desire to uplift children.[49]

Despite the likelihood·of scrutiny from the various con-
stituencies interested in a detailed portrait of educational
practice in an all-black school, Paul did not idealize her community. She underscored James Jackson's commitment to his
schooling but also recounted his victimization by neighborhood truants whose race she did not specify. Perhaps Paul
also recognized that white criticism had some merit: through
editorial asides and compelling anecdotes, she encouraged
her African American readers to value education, to take ad-

vantage of the educational opportunities available to them, and to consider education's uplifting social, intellectual, emotional, and spiritual dimensions.

THE EIGHTY-EIGHT-PAGE 1835 edition of the *Memoir of James Jackson* contains no illustrations, epigraphs, dedications, or any of the authenticating documents that usually accompanied early nineteenth-century African American writings.[50] By comparison to the increasingly popular antebellum slave narratives, the *Memoir* was spartan in both format and content. Without the materials that advocated the narrative's acceptance by the antislavery community, attested to the narrator's experiences, or explained the role of the editor or amanuensis, Paul's narrative was clearly an alternative African American text.

In the preface Paul issues an authoritative statement about the *Memoir*'s veracity: "We most confidently believe there is nothing like exaggeration in any part of the narrative." She continues: "We were permitted to hear a statement of the facts before there was any design of making them public." These words suggest that she was part of an interested group that was privy to a formal testimonial unaffected by the allure and pressures of the literary marketplace. Her statement of authenticity clearly was persuasive to her publisher, who did not insist on obtaining any other imprimatur. It also establishes Paul's commanding voice as biographer, narrator, social critic, and educated free black woman.

The preface also offers the first insights about Paul's sense of her audience. She addresses "all who are candid," "colored friends," and African American "parents and teachers" as she extols the "moral and intellectual powers of colored children." Her first overtures are to an unspecified and presumably educated white audience with antislavery tendencies. Her comments about "unholy prejudice" and the systemic neglect of African American children suggest that for these readers the forthcoming memoir will function as a didactic narrative whose compelling moral message will prompt them to endorse educational reform and social outreach to black children and their families. In the next paragraph Paul addresses her African American audience. The rhetoric of passionate spirituality supersedes the language of polite social protest as she exhorts black communities to invest in their children. To this audience Paul suggests that the *Memoir*'s power lies in its ability to confirm the vital connection between spiritual education and social progress: "let it prompt parents and teachers to store the minds of the children committed to them with religious truth, and God will give you a large reward; yea, a hundred fold. In this life, you shall see your children coming up to be respected in society, and in the world to come, they shall be acknowledged by our Lord as heirs to life eternal." The *Memoir* is meant to encourage African American readers to make or renew their commitment to religious education and spiritual-minded childrearing. Paul's use of direct address in this section underscores her ease with her African American audience, confirming her sense that they have similar concerns about civil rights, morality, and the spiritual welfare of children.[51]

In the preface, Paul directs her comments to adult readers of the *Memoir;* in the narrative proper, however, it is clear that she is also writing for and to another set of readers, children. Her style is modeled on the conventional evangelical pedagogical style of the day; the narrative voice of the twenty-six-year-old teacher is alternately intimate and demanding, quizzing readers about what they have read, outlining catechisms for them to memorize and apply in their daily lives, and soliciting answers about their reactions to the text. More than once she asks her young readers how their home lives compare with that of James Jackson. After relating an episode in which James and his mother pray together, Paul directly engages her juvenile audience: "Did you ever ask your father or mother to go away alone with you, and pray to God for you?" she asks. Her question is not simply rhetorical. She continues: "will you ask them to-night, or to-morrow morning?"

The narrative proper closes with an account of James's last moments in a highly emotional and protracted deathbed scene. "The Little Blind Boy" and "Am I to Blame?," two brief stories with corresponding poems, conclude the volume.[52] Each piece articulates a clear moral and spiritual lesson for its young readers and, like the accounts of James in the *Memoir* proper, encourages self-reflection. These supplementary pieces, typical of the numerous didactic and interrogatory tales published in antebellum American Sunday School Union newspapers and juvenile periodicals, offer additional lessons about charity, acceptance, and good Christian behavior.[53] In the commentary preceding "Am I to Blame?," a poem about "a little boy who was grieved because other boys shunned his company," the narrator encourages her readers to "See what he asks his mother in the last verse" and then asks, "What do you think of the question?" Interrogatories such as these made the text accessible and reinforced its interactive nature. The questions and direct address in these supplementary pieces and throughout the *Memoir* proper encouraged readers to advance in their own spiritual education and moral development.[54]

Throughout, the *Memoir* places James, the moral child of color, rather than Susan Paul, pioneering African American author, before the reading public. Paul takes pains not to distract her readers from his remarkable life and example. She does not dwell on what his life and death meant to her personally. Her primary goals are to allow James to inspire his peers and to encourage them and their parents to recognize the spiritual needs of all American children.

UPON COMPLETING the manuscript, Paul approached two religious organizations, the Baptist Sabbath School Society and the Orthodox Congregational Sabbath School Society, and asked them to print and disseminate her work. Both societies were subsidiaries of the American Sunday School Union (ASSU), a "publisher of formidable productivity" that historians of nineteenth-century print culture have credited with an exceptional investment in and distribution of juvenile literature.[55] Paul's effort to have her work adopted by these influential publishing organizations indicates not only her self-confidence but also her desire to emphasize the spiritual—rather than political or abolitionist—import of her work. This tactical decision also attests to the constraints and categorization that affected African American writers. Of course, if she attracted a religious readership and her work had political overtones, then she succeeded on two fronts, since religious interest often led to political participation. Paul wanted a mainstream market for her work and aspired to gain access to Christian families and readers already targeted by the Sabbath school movement. It was not to be.

The societies Paul approached were part of an organization that sought to remain neutral on one of the most explosive issues of the day: slavery. The ASSU, which had affiliates in all twenty-four states by 1832, was led by increasingly conservative board members, who, in their attempt to create a unified national organization, declared that the issue of slavery and any divisive related issues, such as abolition, must not be mentioned in ASSU publications. Although the Sunday school movement had, since its inception, labored to provide education for "every creature of whatever race, color, or country," proslavery southerners and Sunday school affiliates were wary of what historian Janet Cornelius has referred to as "the liberating aspects of literacy."[56] In the aftermath of the Nat Turner revolt, the ASSU failed to protest the radical reforms of Sabbath school education for enslaved blacks, which often involved a shift away from reading and writing instruction to oral training and rote memorization, and tacitly endorsed the elimination of Sabbath schools for slaves and people of color.

In many southerners' minds, African American literacy was feared as a stepping-stone to civil disobedience.[57] Evidence of this perception emerges in one of Frederick Douglass' experiences as a teacher. In 1833 Douglass organized and began leading a promising Sabbath school for African American children in Maryland. His master and other white Methodist men soon charged that Douglass "wanted to be another Nat Turner," asked whether he wanted to "die the way [Turner] did," and then "raised stout sticks against the scholars and broke up the school."[58] In the same year ASSU managers directed their missionaries to avoid "studiously and constantly . . . the subject of slavery, abolition, and every other irritating topic."[59] The topic and representation of American slavery became anathema to proponents of the institutionalized religious education system advanced by the ASSU. Susan Paul's quest for ASSU patronage coincided with the organization's increasing tolerance of southern racial prejudice, its systematic abandonment of African American students in the South and North, and its documented rejection and censorship of all materials containing references to slavery.[60]

The ASSU affiliates refused to publish the *Memoir* or to stock it at their depositories for distribution to Sabbath schools nationwide.[61] This rejection meant that Paul would not benefit from the organization's lucrative and well-financed juvenile publication market. Perhaps even more discouraging was the society's refusal to distribute the *Memoir*. Sabbath school libraries, an established fixture in the northern communities that Paul wanted to reach, "were not only free, but often the only circulating libraries in a community. They reached many a child who had few other sources of reading material."[62] The *Memoir* would also be excluded from widely disseminated ASSU book catalogues and the lists of books touted as suitable award books for young students. Rebuffed by the central religious juvenile publishing organization of her time, Paul was forced to seek out patronage that was local rather than national, individual rather than institutional, and secular rather than religious.[63]

The details of Paul's publishing frustrations were documented in an anonymous letter to the editor published in *The Liberator* on August 1, 1835. According to the writer, the white Bostonian printer and bookseller James Loring was "anxious that [the *Memoir*] should be printed, paid Miss Paul for the copy-right, and then published it on his own responsibility." The author, who may have been James Loring himself or someone close to Paul who was familiar with the manuscript's history, included a brief excerpt from the text, details about Paul's publishing travails, and a recommendation that "all the *true* friends of the colored people . . . forthwith possess themselves of a copy for their own families, and also take special pains to see that at least one or two copies

are put into the library of their respective Sabbath Schools."
Paul's eloquent advocate closed by asserting: "And now that
it may not be said that I recommend to others what I do not
practice, I will simply add, that recently in a little social
meeting that I attended, I stated the above facts, and the
money for *eighteen copies* of the book was paid down on the
spot, and to-day I have had the pleasure of laying the money
out in purchasing them for the friends who thus advanced the
money. Reader, go thou and do likewise—ay, and better
too."[64]

Loring may well have been Paul's anonymous supporter.
He probably came to know her through their common involvement in civic events devoted to antislavery and racial
uplift. The two shared a common faith as well: she was the
daughter of a Baptist minister, and he was a deacon in the
city's First Baptist Church. On several occasions before
the *Memoir*'s publication, Loring sold tickets at his Washington Street bookstore for Paul's juvenile concerts.[65] In being
published by Loring and stocked at the Massachusetts Anti-
Slavery Society—alongside copies of Maria Stewart's *Productions* (1835) and Phillis Wheatley's collected poems—
Paul's work became part of the specialized political and racial market that she had originally tried to avoid. Yet the
Memoir did not lose its spiritual appeal as a result of these ar-
rangements. Loring printed and sold much religious and didactic children's literature, as well as narratives about race,
ethnicity, and religion.[66] For Susan Paul, Loring's record
would have been further enhanced by his publication in 1832

of the *Memoir of Mrs. Chloe Spear: a native of Africa, who was enslaved in childhood, and died in Boston, January 3, 1815, aged 65 years,* written by "A lady of Boston." Susan Paul may have had only dim memories of the highly respected Mrs. Spear, who died when Susan was six, but their two families had enjoyed particularly close relations up until Spear's death. According to her biographer, Mrs. Spear felt so strongly about Susan's father that "she was much in the habit of calling [him] her *son*."[67]

Paul's influential abolitionist friend William Lloyd Garrison also championed her work. In keeping with its tradition of supporting African American literary efforts, *The Liberator* publicized the *Memoir* and on June 27, 1835, printed two especially didactic excerpts containing anecdotes about Boston children. These selections stressed the book's general appeal and its focus on a variety of children, not just one African American. An editorial note above the excerpts announced: "We make the following extracts from the Memoirs of this little colored boy, written by Miss Susan Paul, and just published by James Loring." Just beneath the excerpts was a list of "Anti Slavery Publications" available at the Massachusetts Anti-Slavery Society. The list included Paul's *Memoir* along with the *Memoir & Poems of Phillis Wheatley* and Lydia Maria Child's *Appeal in favor of that class of Americans called Africans.*[68]

The *Memoir of James Jackson* quickly circulated beyond northeastern abolitionist circles. The Massachusetts Anti-Slavery Society sent a copy to Oberlin College, where it be-

Advertisement for the *Memoir of James Jackson,* for sale at the Massachusetts Anti-Slavery Society bookshop, *The Liberator,* April 15, 1837 came a part of the original library collection.[69] In 1836 another copy was donated to the Yale College Brothers in Unity, one of two popular undergraduate literary and debating societies.[70] Between the mid-1750s and 1872, when the societies disbanded and donated their libraries to the university's general collection, all incoming Yale students belonged to either the Linonia Society or the Brothers in Unity. There are no circulation records for the Brothers in Unity, so it is impossible to determine how many of its members read Paul's book. However, the logbooks documenting the society's weekly debate questions and audience votes reveal that Yale students in the 1830s were interested in questions about slavery, civil rights, equal opportunity, and privilege. As one of the organization's few African American texts, the *Memoir* was an extremely important acquisition for groups "seriously meant, by those who founded them, to supply a kind of literary culture which the curriculum did not furnish." The story of James Jackson was considered important enough to include in "beginnings of a literary life" for Yale College students.[71]

In the *memoir of James Jackson* Susan Paul combines elements of two distinctive nineteenth-century literary forms, the didactic spiritual narrative and the juvenile biography. Frances Foster describes most African American women's writings in the 1830s as "homiletic combinations of autobiography, poetry, and essay. Virtually all of them were informed by an evangelical enthusiasm and authority from the Bible . . . in general these writers assumed the authority and the intention to instruct audiences composed of men and women of all races."[72] The intersection of secular and spiritual tensions in Paul's *Memoir* invites consideration of the popular white literary forms that were the most likely models for Paul and other young women authors.

The didactic juvenile literature in circulation during Paul's young adulthood provided countless examples of young children who were encouraged to and then became responsible for their own moral identity. According to Anne Scott MacLeod, in these works children's characters are "somewhat obscured by [their] exaggerated conscientiousness . . . and by the authors' steady harping on the importance of obedience to parental authority."[73] The *Memoir* conforms to these generic characteristics. Paul reports on James's sensitivity to his mother's domestic chores and his early-developed and extremely heightened sense of responsibility. She notes that young James Jackson was a model child, in whom deliberate sin was practically nonexistent. She frequently cites his exemplary behavior, stating, for instance, that after the age of three, "the time cannot be recollected when he exhibited any considerable degree of stubbornness." Later she muses that "some one who is reading this book will inquire, if James was never a bad boy at school. His teacher cannot recollect that at any time he did what he *knew* was wrong." Paul downplays the likelihood that James, like other children, had temperamental flaws. Her idealized portrait is best understood, however, in the context of evangelical juvenilia, whose generic conventions encouraged such presentations.

The social milieu in which Susan Paul was raised, her

good education, and her carefully structured religious home life suggest that as a girl she was primarily exposed to the "catechetical and moral literature" that featured "trusting and fit child[ren] . . . who responded to the challenge of creating heaven on earth."[74] Later she would undoubtedly have seen the locally printed *Juvenile Miscellany*, a periodical for children that her BFASS colleague Lydia Maria Child edited in Boston from 1826 through 1834.[75] As the child of evangelical parents, Paul would almost certainly have read books inspired by such influential works as James Janeway's *A Token for Children, being an exact account of the conversion, holy and exemplary lives and joyful deaths of several young children* (1672) and John Bunyan's *Pilgrim's Progress* (1678, 1684). Such works about God-fearing children featured holy rather than gruesome deaths, examples of good moral choices, and accounts of young people taking moral responsibility for their thoughts and actions. As Janeway's seventeenth-century title indicates, moral tales usually recounted children's conversion, discussed their applications of their newfound faith, and concluded with details of the children's sobering but inspiring death.[76]

In moral literature and juvenile biography of this period, the subject of death was inextricably bound up with notions of piety and obedience. Gillian Avery proposes that death was a primary subject in the education of evangelical children; "those responsible for their upbringing felt that their most solemn charge was to secure . . . 'early piety,' that is, a change of heart in the child, a realization of his utterly sinful nature, his total depravity."[77] The popular religious literature directed at Christian teachers like Paul asked pointedly whether they had "told [students] of their exposedness to death . . . reminded them of the instances of sudden death, which occur so frequently around us," and asked explicitly whether teachers had "in a manner, which would convince [students] that [they] felt the solemnity of the subject, besought them to make preparation for their great and last change."[78] Given that Paul was both a conscientious Sabbath school teacher and James Jackson's biographer, it is not surprising that she would highlight issues pertaining to James's conceptions of and instruction about death, a sobering but emancipatory aspect of his spiritual education.

In her extended eulogy Paul provides no details of James's spiritual conversion. She uses death, rather than a rejection of sin per se, to confirm his preternatural goodness and enviable civic sensibilities. Paul is neither self-conscious nor apologetic about James's freedom from moral failings. She boldly installs him as an ideal example of upstanding, uncomplicated morality—an example that was unprecedented in contemporary juvenile biography.[79] Paul avoids the thorny issue of whether an African American child could in fact be part of the didactic genre of juvenile literature, incorporated into white American homes and Sunday schools. She transcends this material question by concentrating on the feelings and convictions that confirm James's humanity rather than by dwelling on his racial identity.

Paul embellishes the *Memoir*'s insistent message about

African American humanity, however, by giving substantial
narrative attention to the impact of death on African American familial and social relations. In the opening pages she
pays tribute to James's loving and affectionate relationship
with his father. His father's untimely death meant that he
"had no father to come home at night, and let him climb up
into his lap, and tell him what he had seen and heard that
day." This image of father and son is repeated when Mrs.
Jackson answers her son's first questions about death: "his
mother told him, that his father, whom he used to see in the
house, and in whose lap he used to sit, was in heaven. Then
she said that all good people would go to heaven, and be
happy, and live with God forever: death would not come and
take the father of any away from that place."[80] The examples
of paternal intimacy emphasize that James's initial understanding of death is framed in physical and familial terms.
By the end of the narrative, however, James no longer asso-
ciates death solely with his father or thinks of it as a means to
a reunion with him. Instead, his understanding of and desire
for death as a means by which he can keep company with
Christ proves his spiritual maturity and transcendence and
confirms his piety and worthiness as a model juvenile evangelical figure.

Like other books in the genre, Paul's narrative presents
death as the primary catalyst for James's moral and spiritual
development. At first it seems that James, like the protagonist
Alfrado in Harriet Wilson's 1859 narrative *Our Nig*, desires
to go to heaven in order to preserve a satisfying emotional

relationship. However, this human inclination rapidly subsides as James begins to behave like a young Christ child who is on earth not to mourn the loss of his earthly parent, but to do the work of God, his heavenly Father. Though "so young he could not understand much about death," James "in a very little while . . . asked his mother a great many questions about dying." Eventually "his mind would seem busy in reflection, and he often proposed questions which astonished all who heard them." His precocious spirituality becomes increasingly evident: "Before James was three years old, he had made so many inquiries about heaven, and good people, that he seemed to know, in many things, what God approved, and what he did not." In James's questions and observations about death, election, and eternal life, Paul's Christian readers would recognize her allusion to New Testament accounts of the young Christ baffling the scribes in the temple with his knowledge and confidence.

James's transition from private to public rumination about spiritual matters marks the end of his childlike mourning and the beginning of his spiritual maturation. To mark the transition, Paul inserts herself briefly into the narrative: "We should hesitate to relate these circumstances, if juvenile biography did not furnish many facts, which fully prove that the hearts of those who are very young are often inclined to serious concerns." James's new religious sensibilities do not stem from his rejection of sin and subsequent embrace of God and salvation, as in most conversion narratives. According to Paul, his spiritual maturation is fostered instead by his community. Paul credits James's "great many friends" in that community for encouraging his Christian faith and his educational progress. In so doing, she testifies to their upstanding character as well as to their ambition for this young boy and other children. This exemplary child is a product of a virtuous community: region, class, and race both define and produce James Jackson's identity. He is a black evangel living in the heart of Beacon Hill.

SUSAN PAUL DOCUMENTS the socialization of the African American child in two central nineteenth-century institutions: the home and the church. What makes her account striking is the fact that didactic literature about the American home rarely treated African American homes and churches or offered objective portraits of those environments or the women in them who functioned as agents of moral change and spiritual uplift. Paul's illustrations of James Jackson's public education are mirrored by equally full descriptions of how he benefited from additional instruction from his mother. The narrative documents how female figures like James's mother and teacher functioned as primary moral guides for the children in their care. James's mother plays an integral role, providing her son's teacher and biographer with information about the remarkable child both knew and loved. Paul relies on Mrs. Jackson for details about the child's home life, his reaction to his father's death, and his other family relationships. This information enables her to celebrate the Jacksons' modest dwelling as a credible republican home, a place in which children achieve a moral and spiritual consciousness. In addition, Paul confirms that both she and Mrs. Jackson embody the tenets of evangelical womanhood, a cultural ideal usually attributed to white women and white mothers. The domestic intimacy between Mrs. Jackson and Susan Paul promoted their investments in the symbolic and real American family even as it reinforced their adherence to traditional gender roles.

References to reading practices figure prominently in Paul's depiction of moral education in the African American home and community. James's schooling has an immediate and sustained impact on the quality—moral and emotional—of his home life. Chapter II begins with a brief comment about local school admission policies and then establishes that James's religious home training fueled his desire to attend school:

James never attended the infant school; so that he was not taught much before he was nearly four years old. He had learned to repeat a few verses, and was so very anxious to learn to read, that he used to ask his mother when he should go often to school . . .

When [friends of the family] saw how anxious he was to learn to read, they urged his mother to make application for his admission to the Primary School. Although children of his age are not often admitted into that school, yet because he was so good a boy, and so anxious to begin school, he was admitted before he had learned all his let-

ters. When James knew he was to go to school, he seemed
delighted. "O Ma!" said he, "I shall soon be able to read
the Holy Bible to you."

This account reinforces Paul's earlier descriptions of righteous and respectable African Americans in Boston. The fact
that James learns to repeat Bible verses even before he learns
all his letters suggests his repeated exposure to such material
and the influence of the good-hearted Christian people who
taught it to him. An unidentified "they" (most likely a group
of African American neighbors which may have included
Paul herself) persuade Mrs. Jackson to press for an exception
in the primary school admission policies. James's desire to
learn is repeatedly described as a state of anxiety: in this
short passage alone, the word *anxious* appears three times.
His urgency stems from his desire to read the Bible to his
mother. Subsequent accounts of domestic rituals in the Jackson home confirm that James takes pride in his participation
in a central activity, family Bible reading. James's contribution to this aspect of his home life expands the notion of
what constituted nineteenth-century domesticity in the antebellum homes of free African Americans.

Paul's emphasis on the cooperative public and private efforts to begin James's schooling underscores fundamental
similarities and differences between the northern and southern contexts of African American literacy. Many black children in both the North and the South were educated through
communal, interracial, and intraracial efforts. Paul's *Memoir*

appeared during the increasingly violent backlash against African American education brought on by the Nat Turner revolt and the highly publicized and assaults on Prudence Crandall's Connecticut academy for young women of color in 1834. Even as black communities and white abolitionists continued to promote and protect African Americans' educational rights, some southern legislators were boasting that they had "as far as possible closed every avenue by which light may enter [slaves'] minds. If we could extinguish [their] capacity to see the light, our work would be completed; they would then be on a level with the beasts of the field and we should be safe!"[81]

Even so, slaves did manage to become literate. In *Stolen Childhood*, a pioneering study of slave children, Wilma King notes that in the antebellum South, literacy and spiritual redemption were frequently intertwined and that slaves—and particularly enslaved children—who were exposed to lessons about Christianity ultimately became literate in the process.[82] Paul's presentation of James's Bible-reading sessions at home with his mother, then, was an effective reminder of the connection between literacy, spiritual education, and African American freedom—the combination that proslavery advocates increasingly feared most.

Paul presents African American domesticity as inextricably linked to spiritual sensibilities. In illustrating this connection, she describes a traditional evening of Bible reading between Mrs. Jackson and her young son. The scene is remarkable for its awed, hushed account of spiritualized domestic intimacy between an African American mother and child:

> Sometimes when Mrs. Jackson had been reading in the Bible, and after she had done and put the book by, James would take her by the hand, and lead her away, that she might pray with him alone. Now do you not think that James loved to hear prayer? Did you ever ask your father or mother to go away alone with you, and pray to God for you? will you ask them to-night, or to-morrow morning?

The catechetical questions following the brief account are representative of the conventional Sabbath school pedagogical methods used to impart the fundamental elements of evangelical Christianity. In the *Memoir,* however, the catechism also suggests Susan Paul's confidence that she can bridge the social, cultural, and spiritual divides between white and black American households.[83] In this account she implicitly protests against the exclusion of examples of African American domesticity from American juvenile literature, offering an image of American life that involves African Americans but is worlds apart from slavery. The reading scene highlights exemplary American domesticity but places it squarely within an inspirational testimony to African American spiritual life and practice. In so doing, Paul asserts that young James and his mother are appropriate role models for all American families and that such figures exist in African American homes. Paul was also aware of the degree to which slave parents and children had to be surreptitious in their pursuit of education; in this scene she celebrates the unselfconscious learning process available to free African Americans.

Like many other nineteenth-century writers, Paul venerates the American mother. She refers obliquely to Mrs. Jackson's overwhelming domestic responsibilities as a single parent. She also alludes to her status as a working woman, an unusual detail. However, these remarks are overshadowed by periodic emphases on the more genteel duties that place Mrs. Jackson squarely within a venerated social group: American mothers whose primary responsibility it is to raise moral, upstanding citizens and who do so chiefly by conducting conversations in the home about spiritual matters. Paul confirms that an African American home in an impoverished, segregated black neighborhood can still be an effective site of moral training and spiritual contemplation. Her passionate assertions in this direction make the *Memoir* especially compelling and clearly challenged the Primary School Committee and Sabbath School Society publishers, both of whom essentially refused to acknowledge or emphasize African American morality and exemplary parenting.

Once James enters school, the references to reading practices in the Jackson home multiply. Five substantial references confirm the centrality of religious materials in James's primary school classroom and illuminate how Bible study establishes certain domestic rhythms and provides occasions for intimacy between mother and son: before "James learned all his letters, and began to read in syllables . . . he had

learned several little hymns, which he was very fond of repeating to his mother." Teachers in the African American
schools were establishing seamless links between their classrooms and community churches, apparently using "little
hymns" for their rote memorization exercises. Paul makes no
mention of secular schoolbooks that may have been used in
segregated Boston schoolrooms, and thereby avoids having
to address the problematic ways in which approved public
school texts presented or sidestepped such explosive social issues as slavery and poverty.[84]

The one schoolroom text that Susan Paul mentions in detail is the Bible. Her desire to showcase the substantial spiritual dimensions of African American life may explain this
narrow focus. Yet she does not present the Bible simply as a
spiritual text or revered holy book; it functions also as an example of how to create historical records. She also uses it to
promote the idea that writing is related to one's spiritual responsibilities and that the profession of authorship is in fact
a type of civic duty. In an informative review of African
American antebellum classroom discussions, Paul describes
at length how she introduced students to the Bible and its
major figures: Adam and Eve, Moses, Noah, Jesus, and the
apostles Paul and Peter. In her study of evangelical pedagogy and materials, Anne Boylan notes that Bible stories
such as these established a common Christian acculturation
process for Sabbath school students.[85] This process is clearly
under way in Paul's schoolroom, yet even more striking
about her account of Bible teaching is her emphasis on the

Bible's form. After the tale of the Flood and the earthly wickedness that prompted it, she tells her students a story that stresses the intellectual dimensions of writing:

> After a long time, God directed a man by the name of Moses, to write these things down in a book, so that the people could see how he had punished the disobedient men who lived in that age of the world. So Moses wrote all these things in a book, and the people whom we call Jews, kept this book in their temple. After this, other men wrote what God directed them to. The people had all the writings collected. This made what we call the Old Testament.

She then discusses the New Testament in such a way that it becomes a publication history:

> There was no more writing for a long time, until our blessed Saviour came into the world.[86] Then God commanded those men who were with him to write what the Saviour said, and what he did; so four of them wrote an account of these things. These accounts, together with some of the letters which Paul, Peter and others wrote, make the New Testament; and both together, are called the HOLY BIBLE.

Paul's pedagogy is marked indelibly by her awareness of the importance of social and historical records. The repeated references to writing, commands to write, and the active role of people in preserving written material underscore the teacher's—and most likely the community's—effort to document African Americans' own history of racial oppression and emancipation. Paul emphatically establishes the Bible as a testimonial social text that records the struggles, victories, and cultural practices of groups that included oppressive slave owners and long-suffering slaves, faithful Christians and divinely inspired historians. These powerful facts reinforced Paul's mission to record the life of James Jackson, a young Christian disciple, and they also encouraged African Americans to think about the need for memory books, texts that would preserve their history in much the same way that the Old Testament recorded accounts of the Jews' Egyptian bondage.

Throughout the *Memoir* Paul emphasizes the reciprocal relationship between public and private spheres in the African American community. James's teacher in the public schoolroom and his mother in the private home act in concert for his betterment. James quickly absorbs his lessons by making visual connections between his classroom subjects and objects in his home: "While his teacher was giving [a historical] account of the Bible, James listened and seemed delighted. When he went home, he looked at his mother's Bible, and said to himself, 'That is God's book, now I shall love to hear it read better than ever I did before.'" After a few months at school James displays "an increased attachment to the Bible, and the instruction which he had received about the Saviour, produced much effect on him . . . His mind seemed to expand every day, and every day he seemed to be more under the influence of what he had been taught from the blessed book." Soon afterward he is able to make sophisticated connections and to voice them. These philosophical and oral skills certify his ability to minister within his home and community:

> When the class had done reading, the teacher explained this portion of Scripture. James's eyes sparkled with joy when she told the children, that they might go to the Saviour now, by prayer, and he would bless them. After he went home, he told his mother how the Saviour rebuked his disciples, and said, when they told the people not to bring their children to him, Suffer little children to come to me, and forbid them not, for such is the kingdom of heaven. "O mother," said James, "how good the blessed Saviour was, to take *such little children* up, and bless them! I love the Saviour: my teacher says, if I pray to him he will give me a new heart, and then I shall wish to be good, therefore I shall be happy."

Shortly after this account of James's interpretive skills, Paul refers to him as a "little *preacher* [who] was sometimes very earnest in his exhortations [and] seldom failed to gain the attention of those who were about him." She reports that "James loved to pray," that "in his seasons of devotion he was regular, at least night and morning," and that "he used sometimes to take the other children away and pray with them, and talk with them about the blessed Saviour's dying for them, and endeavor to persuade them to be good and love the Lord." James becomes an evangelical teacher among his peers. His impromptu religious services usually follow a particular ritual: "After an affectionate and earnest appeal to his little auditory, he would sometimes sing an appropriate hymn, and always closed with a prayer, for God's blessing upon them." His ministry is not limited to juvenile audiences: "Persons of maturer years were surprised at the appropriate and impressive addresses which he sometimes made." James's precocious spirituality makes him a member of the larger evangelical system. He travels from one sphere to another but always carries his lessons home, where he essentially reestablishes the teacher-student relationship with his mother. In documenting James's transcendent capabilities, Paul establishes a parallel between him and the Christ child whose parents found him teaching in the synagogue.

THE *MEMOIR OF JAMES JACKSON* presents a number of defining moments in the life of an American child. James is exposed to sobering daily realities such as poverty and sickness, as well as other children's disobedience and disrespect, but all such experiences intensify his faith and desire to improve the world. Eventually, however, Paul moves from universal human experiences to one that has particular relevance for young African American children: slavery. Despite Paul's relative reserve as she explains slavery to her primary school students, James's capacity for transcendence is threatened by the knowledge of bondage, and his physical decline is symbolically hastened. The *Memoir* reminds readers that the issues associated with race and slavery transcend region. Paul defies the existing script for early American race literature by presenting an uplifting chronicle of free African Americans and their urban life and community rather than a fictional account of African American experiences in relation to slavery. Relying on documented facts rather than imaginary circumstances, the narrative constitutes the first extended testament to the moral potential and example of real African American children.

Although many works of juvenilia addressed slavery and abolition between 1825 and 1870, the overwhelming majority of the heroic children in these narratives were white.[87] In the *Memoir* Paul redresses this imbalance: she focuses completely on an African American protagonist. She incorporates whites only once. She relates an incident witnessed by a male friend, in which a young white girl threatened the little boy in her charge: "Henry, if you don't be still crying, I will carry you down to Belknap-street, and give you to the *old black man*." The friend who witnessed the event lamented to Paul, "That child will *fear* and *hate* a black man for years. Manhood will scarcely efface his hatred." The few traditional (and white-authored) antislavery texts that featured African American characters did not directly challenge white stereotypes of African Americans or their communities. In her anecdote in the *Memoir*, Paul establishes new terms of racial engagement for white children and their families by offering a substantial biography of a real black child and a new view of African Americans and their communities.

The *Memoir of James Jackson* goes beyond the parameters of contemporary juvenile literature not only in its choice of characters but also in its focus on race rather than slavery as the central issue. The word *slavery* does not appear until the last third the book. Whereas much antislavery and abolitionist juvenile fiction relies on melodramatic scenes of kidnapping, escape, or heart-wrenching family separations, Paul focuses on how slavery affected even free black children. This crucial lesson occurs in her account of how she told the children about slavery:

> One day while at school, his teacher told the children that there were a great many thousands of their color who were not allowed to read, who had no schools, nor any books. These persons she said were slaves. The fathers and mothers of a *great great* many children could not do as they pleased with them, because other men said that they could sell them or do what they pleased with them; they are called slaves. These men did not want the slaves to know any thing about reading the Bible. So they kept the children from school, and while you are at school they make the slaves work very hard, and because they don't know any thing at all about the word of God they are sometimes very wicked. Then they are cruelly whipped. So they live and die without ever going to school, or being taught by kind Sabbath school teachers.

Though establishing a racial connection between her pupils and southern slaves, Paul also draws a crucial distinction and in doing so gives her young charges an accessible way to re-assure themselves of their own free condition: they have Sabbath school teachers and access to books and schools;[88] if they attend school, then they are not slaves. Their educa-tion—intellectual, spiritual, and moral—is an indicator and result of liberty.[89] Paul's explanation encourages youngsters in places such as Boston Primary School Number 6 to trea-sure their opportunity to learn and to use it as a way to se-cure their identity as free people. Given Paul's report in 1836 that some of her students were former slaves,[90] it is likely that some were also enrolled during James's attendance in the early 1830s. Paul's elaboration of what slavery prevents—and what freedom ensures—would help such children to es-tablish their new status and rights.

Instead of offering her own critique of proslavery ac-commodationism, Paul presents the emotional reaction of James Jackson, an apparently innocent—read apolitical—child:

When James went home, he said to his mother, "Mother, I have heard to-day about the poor slaves," and "my teacher said, we might pray for them; now Ma, how shall I pray?" "O James," said she, "your teacher has told you much about them,—ask for them just what you think they need." After a few moments of reflection James retired, and was heard to offer the following simple prayer with much feeling. "O Lord, pity the poor slaves, and let them be free, that they may have their liberty, and be as happy as I am,—and may they have good teachers to learn them to read, as I have, and make them all very good. Amen."

James's withdrawal to pray for the slaves is both literal and symbolic; thereafter he never holds spontaneous religious services. Faced with the enormity of slavery's constraints on people of color, people he understands to be like himself, he turns from evangelical exhortation to prayers for earthly improvements as if these are the most pressing changes to be made. As a result of learning about slavery, James no longer regards his life as one in process but rather as one privileged and complete.

Paul represents James's response to slavery as one of withdrawal rather than activism. She adheres to the conventions of evangelical juvenilia in presenting her child hero as an educator and savior and in proposing that a child's innocence could overcome the learned vices of pride and arrogance. James Jackson's career of public intervention, spiritual succor, and mentoring peaks long before slavery is mentioned in his classroom or in the *Memoir*. Once he learns about racial oppression, institutionalized disfranchisement, and enforced ignorance, the young evangelist experiences a devastating social death. Paul subtly suggests that in his death shortly afterward James succumbs not to physical illness but rather to the awful social sickness that is slavery. His painful involuntary contortions appear to be a sympathetic response to the fact that most of his fellow African Americans are unable to control their own bodies.[91] He can, however, control the future of his soul and does so by dying and abandoning his vulnerable body.

In nineteenth-century juvenile literature, death is inextricably bound up with the issues of good and evil, innocence and sin. For Susan Paul, death is also—however indirectly— linked to sanctioned oppression and frustrated spirituality. Gillian Avery proposes that in early tract stories, "the death of the central character is necessary to convert the remaining characters. The child's death is a holy example."[92] Yet on the threshold of this monumental event Paul departs dramatically from the conventions of juvenile fiction and pursues a new narrative avenue that in no way depends on contrived symbolism: she documents in detail James's painful sickness and death. Her stirring account is in part an eyewitness account. James fainted in his classroom, was "carried home," where he lapsed into "a state of insensibility, and soon after was seized with violent convulsions, which continued all night with but short intervals. His distress was very great. His limbs were drawn into almost every possible position. He could not speak during all of this great distress." Over two days he experienced a rapid decline: "His fever had raged to such a degree that his thirst was great, and he often called for water"; he "suffered" "repeated convulsions" that "made his flesh exceedingly sore, so that any movement caused him great pain"; and "sometimes a half suppressed groan would escape him, in spite of all his efforts." Paul notes every stage of James's sickness and treatment, referring often to his exhaustion, pain, and endurance. Several times, she tells us, he lost consciousness. However, the first time he "revived . . . and . . . could speak aloud, he exclaimed, 'Glory, honour, praise and power, be unto the Lamb for ever and ever.'"

James's capacity for testimonial utterances—whether he is conscious of them or not—cues Paul's readers to think of the deathbed scene as happy and edifying rather than dreadful. The gathering of his mother, teacher, minister, and doctor around his bed rendered the scene familiar for contemporary readers of juvenile and sentimental fiction. Yet in Paul's account of James Jackson's actual passing there are important departures from conventional deathbed scenes. First, although it is apparent that James's death and his own rationalization of it represent his revulsion at the wickedness of the world, Paul does not stress that James, like so many fictional characters, has "to die because [he has] advanced too far on the road to sanctity for life in this world to be any longer possible for [him]."[93] In keeping with her primary objective to document the life of an American child, Paul stresses James's identity as a child, son, and evangel rather than as a representative of his race. His final moments are private and intimate: he attempts to establish no public record of his short life and spiritual convictions.

James conceives of death as his own prerogative, a transition with no implications for his school-age peers or the larger Boston community. His teacher Susan Paul attempts to draw his attention to the larger world and also gives him the opportunity to generate an inspirational statement for that world when she asks him if he is "willing . . . to leave the school, and . . . teacher and . . . mother." Without hesitation James replies:

> "Yes, I am willing to die; for then I shall go to the blessed Saviour, and I want to be with him, for he said, Suffer little children to come to me, and forbid them not, for of such is the kingdom of heaven." He then commenced singing a hymn, which he had learned at school, which described the Saviour blessing the little children whom he had called to him.
>
> After singing this, he remained silent a few moments, with his eyes apparently fixed on something above him.
>
> He seemed to feel very deeply, for he raised his hand toward heaven and said, "O God, that was *my dear* Saviour who said that. I want to go away and be with him. O, I want to go away from this wicked world, and live always with the blessed Saviour in heaven. There is nothing wicked there."

James's death, as Susan Paul describes it, is a way for him to leave the world's wickedness behind. In what amounts to his last testimony, James reiterates that the wickedness of the world is fueling his desire not simply to die but to live elsewhere. Unlike the usual portrayals of juvenile death scenes as "the natural culmination of the progress to perfection,"[94] Paul suggests through the boy's own words that his death is unnatural, hastened by his exposure to slavery's devastating spiritual oppression. It is the image of James succumbing to rather than transcending wickedness—read slavery—that generates the narrative's true climax and calls for social change and racial uplift.

Once she establishes the reason behind James's fervent desire to die, Paul presents a characteristic Victorian death scene, incorporating recognizable elements of antebellum consolation literature. She uses conventional references to bright light, angels, and the final euphoria of the dying: "His eyes began to grow dim, his hands were cold, and in a few moments all was calm; the glazed eyes of this dear child once more beamed forth with unspeakable delight, and he exclaimed, 'This is God my Saviour; O Lord, this is Jesus.'— His eyes closed, his heart ceased to beat, and all was still. James was dead. Nothing remained but a cold and lifeless lump of clay." This scene, like many other nineteenth-century accounts of death, assures readers that there is indeed an accessible and restorative place called heaven.[95] James's last vision and final words confirm his acceptance in the afterworld, a place to which he is drawn because no one is held in bondage there. Heaven, for James Jackson, is a realm of reunion and continued experience of the spiritual joys he began to taste in his brief earthly life.

The *Massachusetts Vital Records* notes the death, on October 30, 1833, of a seven-year-old "colored" boy named George Jackson, from a "bursting blood vessel."[96] Although the name is incorrect, the date of death is the same as that given in the obituary notice for James Jackson in *The Liberator* (not October 31, as specified in the title of the *Memoir*).

Paris papers of the 21st announce the arrival of our Minister, Mr Livingston, in that city.—It was computed that the removal of the Obelisk from Thebes to Paris, which is now prosecuting, will cost two million and an half francs.—It is positively asserted that Lord Wellesley is to be the last Lord Lieutenant of Ireland. The office, when his lordship retires, is to be abolished, by which £100,000 per annum will be saved to the country.—The celebrated Sir John Stephenson, the composer of the Irish Melodies, died at Meath, on the 14th of September.—His Majesty's brig Trinculo, Lieutenant Thompson, acting, has captured near the Gallena, after a chase of four hours, the Spanish schooner Segunda, with 307 slaves on board. —The cost of the projected railroad from London to Brighton, is estimated at £825,000, and the income at £125,000 a year.—The English papers speak of the harvest as a good one; a full average crop of grain has been gathered, in excellent condition.—A great military review is to take place at Verona, of the troops of Austria and Prussia. A large Austrian force, consisting of 90,000 men, with 300 pieces of cannon, is assembling in the environs of Mantua.—It is reported that the British Government has granted £1000 per annum, towards the support of the Methodist Missionaries in Canada.—It is said that Charles X and the Duchess de Angouleme have refused to receive the Duchess de Berri, or permit her to reside for a time with her children.—A Russian 74 had been beaten on the coast of Finland, and out of a crew of 750 men, 15 only were saved.—Rammohun Roy, the celebrated Brahmin, lately died at Stapleton Grove, near Bristol.

☞ At the Boston Mutual Lyceum, West Centre-Street, the following question will be discussed on MONDAY EVENING NEXT. ' What are the best means to adopt, to remove the prejudice which exists against the people of color ? '

DIED—In this city, Oct. 30, James Jackson, jr., aged 7.

Obituary of James Jackson Jr., *The Liberator*,
November 9, 1833

Immediately after reporting his death, Paul capitalizes on the emotional vulnerability of her readers. She reiterates James's humanity and his cultivated spirituality:

> Now you have read all I have to say about James: you see how obediently he lived, and how happily he died. What do you remember particularly that you have read about him in this book?
>
> Do you wish to be happy? Then you must be good; and you can't be good without trying, and sometimes trying very hard too. Do you think it was easy for James to be kind to boys who were unkind to him? If it was, then it may be easy for you.

If his readers can recognize either James's humanity or his spirituality, Paul suggests, then James can function for them as a legitimate American heroic figure. In the remaining pages of the book she eulogizes an exemplary American child whose behavior bridges racial and social divides. As James Jackson's biographer, Paul tries to use the boy's life as a good son, "attentive and obedient scholar," and young Christian to promote positive domestic change:

> Now do you remember the words written in large letters which [James] used to think of so often? I will write them again here, so that you can find them easily when you want to look at them. Here they are:
>
> THOU, GOD, SEEST ME!
>
> LOVE YOUR ENEMIES;—AND
>
> DO TO OTHERS AS YOU WISH OTHERS TO DO TO YOU.

If you remember the first line, which I have written in large letters, you will not be inclined to do what you are forbidden to do by your parents, if they *are* out of your sight.

When you think of the second, you will not be inclined to injure those who have done wrong to you.

And if you always recollect the last, you will not injure any person who is poor, or in distress, or colored.

Paul stresses God's commandments in order to promote her readers' self-consciousness while they are children and as they become young adults. Early in the *Memoir* Paul provided an anecdotal account of young white Bostonians responding to and reinforcing racial stereotypes. In this final chapter, Paul uses words from the Bible and James's example to compel more responsible and sensitive behavior in her white readers, young and old alike. In her interpretive review of God's commandments, Paul links each one to a familial, personal, and community issue. This series of injunctions reinforces her consistent message about James Jackson's experience of home, school, and community. In closing, Paul simultaneously draws ambitious national and domestic implications from a tale with an essentially conventional plot. What sets this story apart is its protagonist: a Negro child who is extremely good and ennobling.

THE DIDACTIC FICTION in circulation in the late 1820s and the 1830s included numerous accounts of extremely conscientious children for whom morality and holiness were paramount.[97] The juvenile hero of Susan Paul's *Memoir* achieves this state of mind but ultimately succumbs to death because other Americans do not take responsibility for the state of their own souls. In chronicling James Jackson's life and death, Paul advocates social and moral change by inviting readers to honor her student's life and pain. In addition to details about James Jackson's efforts to develop his spirituality, Paul provides practical pedagogical models for white teachers to implement in their classrooms, homes, and communities.

For the *Memoir* to succeed, its didacticism and series of loving accounts of James's life and death had to encourage in young children humanistic sentiments and sensitivity to poverty, abuse, racial stereotypes, and slavery. In order to accomplish this, Paul adhered to conventions of spiritual narrative and juvenile biography as she blended accounts of James's schooling, home life, and social experiences in Boston. But as Paul revised certain conventions of white antislavery juvenile literature she did not obscure slavery and issues of oppression. This didactic tale became an exercise in generic innovation as she addressed controversial contemporary issues such as slavery, racial hysteria, and racial stereotypes. Paul gained a wider audience for her analyses of these matters by incorporating them into an exemplary evangelical tale.

Susan Paul's ambitious goal was to introduce African American domesticity, religious practice, spiritual development, morality, and ethics to American readers. She transformed divisive topics into palatable, evocative narratives of human development and socialization. Whatever her success in attaining her goal, Paul's work merits critical attention today because it provides invaluable documentation of African American reading practices, moral education in the home, segregated schools, and African American Sabbath schools. Finally, it shows how an early African American writer challenged the essentialist notion that slavery was the primary and most suitable context for narratives about African American life.

In 1835 the *Memoir of James Jackson* was hailed as "a simple memoir, not of a party character, thoroughly evangelical in its sentiments and written in a style that would do honor to any lady in the land."[98] Today we might also add that the *Memoir* is an invaluable record of African American socialization and female advocacy.

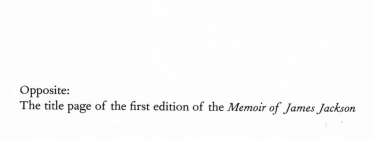

Opposite:
The title page of the first edition of the *Memoir of James Jackson*

MEMOIR

OF

JAMES JACKSON,

THE ATTENTIVE
AND OBEDIENT SCHOLAR,

WHO DIED IN BOSTON, OCTOBER 31, 1833, AGED SIX
YEARS AND ELEVEN MONTHS.

BY HIS TEACHER,
MISS SUSAN PAUL.

BOSTON:
PUBLISHED BY JAMES LORING,
132 Washington Street.

1835.

PREFACE

The design of this Memoir is, to present the incidents in the life of a little colored boy. The circumstances in which he was placed, the first four years of his life, rendered it impracticable for the writer to present as many particulars as might be deemed desirable. It was thought better to diminish the fullness of incident, rather than the authenticity of the statements. We most confidently believe there is nothing like exaggeration in any part of the narrative. We were permitted to hear a statement of the facts before there was any design of making them public.

There is, surely, sufficient in this little book to convince all who are candid, that the moral and intellectual powers of colored children are inferior to the power of others, only as their advantages are inferior. Let, then, this little book do something towards breaking down that unholy prejudice which exists against color. These children of our brethren have too long been neglected. There is among them many a gem, and whose is the guilt that they are not brought out from among the rubbish and polished?

Should this book fall into the hands of our colored friends, let it prompt parents and teachers to store the minds of the children committed to them with religious truth, and God will give you a large reward; yea, a hundred fold. In this life, you shall see your children coming up to be respected in society, and in the world to come, they shall be acknowledged by our Lord as heirs to life eternal. If you will labor in this way, your reward is certain, for the Lord has promised it. May he impart grace to us all to labor for, and, if need be, to suffer with him. Then shall we reign with Him in his kingdom forever.

CHAPTER I

MY DEAR CHILDREN,

I am going to tell you in this book about a little boy. His parents lived in Boston, and the name of his father was James Jackson, a respectable coloured man. This little boy was born on the fifth of December, 1826; and was called James, as his father was.

While very small, James enjoyed excellent health, and appeared to have a mild and pleasant disposition. He was not much more than one year old, when he showed a very strong attachment to his father and mother. But before James was two years old, his father was taken sick, and after suffering a great deal he died. Then James had no father to come home at night, and let him climb up into his lap, and tell him what he had seen and heard that day.

James was so young he could not understand much about death; but in a very little while he asked his mother a great many questions about dying. He inquired where people went when they died; and if all went to one place. So one day his mother told him, that his father, whom he used to see in the house, and in whose lap he used to sit, was in heaven. Then she said that all good people would go to heaven, and be happy, and live with God forever: death would not come and take the father of any away from that place.

James remembered his father, and he loved to think of him; so after his mother had told him these things, he would think that he must die as his father had, but then if I am good, he would say, I shall go where he is.

Long after one of these conversations with his mother, his mind would seem busy in reflection, and he often proposed questions which astonished all who heard them.

We should hesitate to relate these circumstances, if juvenile biography did not furnish many facts, which fully prove that the hearts of those who are very young are often inclined to serious concerns. We feel deep gratitude to Him who hath the hearts of children in his hands, that we may add these facts to the ample testimony of the goodness of our heavenly Father.

Before James was three years old, he had made so many inquiries about heaven, and good people, that he seemed to know, in many things, what God approved, and what he did not. And he always tried to *do* as well as he knew how. After he was three years old, the time cannot be recollected when he exhibited any considerable degree of stubbornness. Whatever his mother directed, he would do, even if it was to part with his little playthings and toys. *He* was never happier than when he made *others* happy. I wish some of you who read this could see how his eyes would sparkle with pleasure, when he thought he had pleased his dear mother. I am sure you would be sorry that you had given your parents any unnecessary trouble, or spoken unkind words to them, when they desired you to do any thing for them. Your parents always know better than you do what is best for you. Although James was so very young, *he* knew this, and always cheerfully obeyed his mother's commands.

Any of you, my dear children, would have been pleased to have seen little James, only three years old, running about so happy, and so kindly telling his mother some little tale; or if she was not at work, coming and asking something about his dear father who died, or about heaven, or the great God who, he said, gave *him every thing he had*. Then he would seem so happy, and say, "O Ma, I mean to be a good, a *very* good boy." Then he would kiss his mother, and get down from her lap, and sit down and *think* about what his mother had said.

Now I think all good children will say that James was a good boy, and they would like to have seen him. Perhaps some one may dislike him because he was coloured. I would ask if James was not *good;* his having a dark skin does not make him *bad*. It is the *conduct* that makes the boys or men or women bad. *God* has made them all, and loves all that are good, and so should *we* always have courage enough to love any body who is good. Would you love your sister or brother less because they had black or brown hair? or your father or mother because one had black eyes and the other blue eyes? No, I am sure you would not love them any the less.

I will tell you a reason why children do not like coloured people. The anecdote was related to me the other day by a gentleman who saw and heard what I am going to tell you. He said, "As I was passing through one of the most pleasant streets in Boston, my attention was attracted by the crying of a child at some distance before me in the same street. I quick-ened my pace, and soon came sufficiently near to see that there was a little boy and girl under the charge of a girl con-siderably older than either of them. When I came near, I saw that the boy trembled and appeared to be much frightened, as I passed them. The large girl said, 'Henry, if you don't be still crying, I will carry you down to Belknap-street, and give you to the *old black man.*' The poor little fellow put his hand on his mouth, and tried with all his might to stop, but he was so much afraid that he could not. So Sally kept repeating, 'Now if you don't stop, I *will certainly* give you to the *old black man.*' Then Henry looked behind him, and all about, as though he thought the hand of some frightful old creature was just about to take hold of him, and carry him away to a dreadful place. "Ah!" said my friend, "*there* is the reason of prejudice against colour. That child will *fear* and *hate* a black man for years. Manhood will scarcely efface his hatred."

You see, my little reader, that Henry was made to fear a black man, just as you would fear a bear or a serpent. Our blessed Saviour has instructed us to love every body who is good. The Jews used to hate him, because he would talk with, and be kind to those whom they wickedly despised.

In the next chapter I will relate some things that took place about the time James began to go to school.

CHAPTER II

In Boston, children are not admitted to the Primary Schools, until they are four years old, but before they are of that age, they are sometimes sent to an infant school. James never attended the infant school; so that he was not taught much before he was nearly four years old. He had learned to repeat a few verses, and was so very anxious to learn to read, that he used to ask his mother when he should go often to school. The good behaviour of James made him a great many friends.

When they saw how anxious he was to learn to read, they urged his mother to make application for his admission to the Primary School. Although children of his age are not often admitted into that school, yet because he was so good a boy, and so anxious to begin school, he was admitted before he had learned all his letters. When James knew he was to go to school, he seemed delighted. "O Ma!" said he, "I shall soon be able to read the Holy Bible to you."

On his admission to school, his teacher soon discovered that an uncommonly interesting child was committed to her care. He was so ready to obey all that she told him, and so attentive to what she taught, and so kind to all the children, that his teacher, and all the good children, loved him very much.

In a very short time, James learned all his letters, and began to read in syllables. But before this, he had learned several little hymns, which he was very fond of repeating to his mother. When he learned a hymn, that told what was wicked and what was good, he always remembered it, and did just what that told him was right. He sometimes saw bad boys quarrel, and strike each other; this made James sorrowful, for he had learned the verse that said, "our little hands were not made for such a wicked use,"[1] and he had heard his mother read in the Bible, that the eye of God sees children in every place.[2] James loved to think that God, as his heavenly Father, looked down and saw all that he wanted, and he would have been exceedingly sorry to do any thing which would displease so kind and merciful a Father.

There are some children who are six or eight years of age, who have to be told a thing a great many times, and then they say, "I can't repeat it, O I have forgotten it." Now James Jackson scarcely ever did so; but when his teacher said, "James, do you remember what I told you yesterday or this morning?" He would say, "Yes!" and then repeat it to her. Now what do you suppose the reason is, that you forget more easily than James? I will tell you—he attended *very carefully* to what was told him, and kept saying it over to himself. O I wish some of you could see him, when his teacher was repeating some little verse, or some story from the Bible. His eyes would be fixed on her all the time so carefully, that no noise would turn them away. Then when she had done, you might see him looking steadily at something, as if he was trying to retain in his memory what she had said.

One afternoon, while his teacher was conversing with the

children about God and heaven, James was desirous to hear something about the Bible, which he had heard his mother read to him. So she told him how God made the world in which we live, and that he made the sun which shines upon us, and gives us light. After he had made all these things, he made a man whom he called Adam, and a woman whom he called Eve.[3] After Adam and Eve had lived a great many years, they died; and some of their children became very wicked, and did not love God, nor do as he commanded them to do. So God caused it to rain a long time, till all the people in the world, except eight, were drowned.[4] After a long time, God directed a man by the name of Moses, to write these things down in a book, so that the people could see how he had punished the disobedient men who lived in that age of the world. So Moses wrote all these things in a book, and the people whom we call Jews, kept this book in their temple.[5] After this, other men wrote what God directed them to. The people had all the writings collected. This made what we call the Old Testament.

There was no more writing for a long time, until our blessed Saviour came into the world. Then God commanded those men who were with *him* to write what the Saviour said, and what he did; so four of them wrote an account of these things.[6] These accounts, together with some of the letters which Paul, Peter and others wrote, make the New Testament; and both together, are called the HOLY BIBLE. This blessed book tells us what we must do to please God, and much about our Lord and Saviour Jesus Christ. So you should always hear it read with much attention, and do as it directs.

While his teacher was giving this account of the Bible, James listened and seemed delighted. When he went home, he looked at his mother's Bible, and said to himself, "That is God's book, now I shall love to hear it read better than ever I did before." Ever after this, when his mother read the Bible, James placed his little chair close by his mother, and listened to all that was read, with the most perfect silence. Sometimes his brothers or sisters did not attend to what was read, or they would be whispering or making some other noise. This used to make James very uneasy, and he would often affectionately say to them, "O hear, hear what mother reads in the good Bible!"

I wonder what little James would have said, if he had seen how some of the boys and girls who read this book do, while *their* father is reading the Holy Scriptures, or while he is praying to God, their kind benefactor. There are some children who will not sit still, nor listen to a word that is read. Our heavenly Father loves those children who listen attentively to his holy word when their parents read it; and when their parents pray to him, he loves to see them lift up their hearts to their Creator, and join with them in prayer while they ask for God to bless them, and make them good and happy children.

There was once a very good little girl in a Sabbath school, whose father did not love God, I suppose, for he did not pray to him in his family at night or in the morning. After this little girl had been at the Sabbath school some time, one Monday morning, after breakfast, she asked her father if he would not read the Bible, and *talk* to their heavenly Father, as the Sabbath school teacher did. You see how all *good* children love to hear prayer. Do you love to hear people pray to the great God?

I suppose some one who is reading this book will inquire, if James was never a bad boy at school. His teacher cannot recollect that at any time he did what he *knew* was wrong. When he knew what his teacher wanted, he seemed to look forward, that he might not trouble her to repeat what she had before said to him. Every day he became more attached to the school, and seemed every day to love his teacher better. He said he loved his teacher because she taught him to read, and told much about the great God.

Every quarter's schooling gave increasing evidence that the uncommonly strong and ready mind of James was under the influence of what we must call *religious principle*. His mother observed an increasing delight in him, whenever she read to him from the Bible. He could now understand some parts of it much better than he could one year before. From his first beginning to talk, he always offered prayer before he retired to rest. If he was wearied, or a little unwell, the other children could not persuade him to retire without first praying to his heavenly Father. Perhaps all little children who read this, pray, but some of you neglect it occasionally, and sometimes do not *love* to pray, but do it because they are told to. James always appeared to love to pray.

Sometimes when Mrs. Jackson had been reading in the Bible, and after she had done and put the book by, James would take her by the hand, and lead her away, that she might pray with him alone. Now do you not think that James loved to hear prayer? Did you ever ask your father or mother to go away alone with you, and pray to God for you? will you ask them to-night, or to-morrow morning?

CHAPTER III

The amiable disposition of James, made his friends much attached to him. They often gave him little presents of toys, or
fruits. Whatever he had that he could divide, was always
shared among the other children at home, or his companions
at school. He appeared very happy when he was making distribution of his little presents. This was benevolence. There
were *other* boys in school who were *selfish,* that is, they did
not care about making others happy; so that when they had
received any little present from a kind friend, you might hear
them saying to some of the children, "you shall not have any
of this," or "this is mine, you have not got any, and I will not
give you any of mine." I have told you that James appeared
very happy while he was distributing his little presents, but
the selfish boy did not appear to be happy, for he looked ill
natured, as if he did not love any body. There is one short
verse that the blessed Saviour repeated to those that used to
be with him, which James kept in his mind, and acted as it
told him to act. Now if you will remember it, I will write it
down in large letters. These are the words, *Do unto others as
you wish them to do unto you.*[7]

James remembered this one day, when he saw a poor
woman in the street. This woman was old, and very feeble,
and her clothes were ragged. As she walked slowly along,
with her cane, a great many boys collected about her, some
said wicked things, others threw dirt and stones at the poor

woman, but when James saw all this, he ran home crying, and said to his mother, "O mother, does not the great God see those wicked boys?" James thought of the poor woman's distress, and said to himself, "If I was poor and old and had no food, I should want some one, who had plenty of all these things, to give me some of them." So he thought what he could do for her to make her comfortable. Now this was doing unto others as you would wish others to do unto you. If every one would obey this precept as they ought, no person would be despised or abused because they are poor, or because they had a dark skin, nor for any other reason but because they are bad, and even then, we should pity and not despise them.

Sometimes James was reproached, because he was not more fond of play; and persons who visited his mother would inquire, if he was not unwell. When they were gone, James would say, "Mother, I wonder why those people think children should always be playing! I prefer staying with you to playing with bad boys. Do you wish to stay alone now, mother?" When she said yes, he would leave the room, but if he knew that she was alone at work, James would soon be in again. When his mother was very busy, he would often ask, "Mother, what can I do to help you?" If she was not too busy, he improved these opportunities to ask questions about many things, but generally something about his book, or God, or heaven.

He would at such time tell his mother what he had heard boys say, or what he had seen them do, and then ask whether that was right. When his mother said it was not right, James would always take care never to do that wicked thing, or say that wicked word. I know there are some unruly children who hear profane persons say bad words, and thus learn to imitate their conversation, when their parents would know nothing of it. You must remember, that the great God can see you and hear you always. I will mention four words, which I wish you to treasure up in your memory, and frequently repeat to yourselves, when wicked children would lead you into temptation; the words are *Thou God seest me.*[8] In the next chapter, I shall give some account of a little girl, who was taught these words.

CHAPTER IV

I will now tell you of a little girl, by the name of Nancy, only four years old, who so fully believes that God is always present, and continually sees her, that she is kept from fear, when alone or in the dark. There was a gentleman, who lived in the same house with Nancy, who loved her very much; so he used to tell her how God took care of us all in the day time and in the dark night. He told her that God takes care of the little birds that sleep in the trees, and the lambs that play in the field; and then he told her that God is every where, and that he loves all good children, and will take care of them. He knows when Nancy, and all children do wrong, and when they do right. One evening, this gentleman said to Nancy, "Will you go into the parlor in the dark, and bring me my pocket handkerchief?" Then she said, "Is God there in the dark?" He told her that God was there, and in all places. "Then I will go," said she. She went alone, and *felt* in one chair after another, until she found the handkerchief; then she brought it out and said, "From this time I am determined that I will not be afraid, for God is in all places." This little girl appeared after this very happy, because she knew there was a great and good God who always saw her. James Jackson felt just so; and when bad boys tried to make him do wickedly, he would say, "No, I cannot do thus," he would say to himself, "for thou, God, seest me."

When James had attended school only a few months, there

appeared an increased attachment to the Bible, and the in-struction which he had received about the Saviour, produced much effect on him. He had not previously had much careful teaching from his mother, for her family was larger and her cares were so numerous as to prevent giving that attention to James which she desired to give him. His mind seemed to ex-pand every day, and every day he seemed to be more under the influence of what he had been taught from the blessed book.

As his teacher witnessed this increasing attachment to her and his books, she felt more deeply the importance of im-parting to him those principles which the Gospel exhibits. And what she imparted was not lost. The impressions made by particular conversations seemed never to be effaced. Dur-ing the first year which James attended school, he learned more than many children do in three. He was now about five years old, and had been in school more than a year. Every month his attachment to his school increased. He not only exhibited his love to his teacher by obedience and attention to what she said, but often brought her little presents of fruits or flowers, as though he would make some compensa-tion for her instruction. At school, he showed the same love for the Bible, which he did at home. When the class read in the Testament, James always listened with the most fixed at-tention; and when his teacher made any remarks, or ex-plained what was read, James would repeat the words which she spoke, so that he might remember them. One day the class read about our Lord's *blessing* children, in the 19th chapter of Matthew, in the 13th, 14th, and 15th verses: "Then were brought to him little children that he should put his hands on them and pray, and his disciples rebuked them. But Jesus said, Suffer little children to come unto me, and forbid them not, for of such is the kingdom of heaven. And he laid his hands on them and departed."

When the class had done reading, the teacher explained this portion of Scripture. James's eyes sparkled with joy when she told the children, that they might go to the Saviour now, by prayer, and he would bless them. After he went home, he told his mother how the Saviour rebuked his disciples, and said, when they told the people not to bring their children to him, Suffer little children to come to me, and forbid them not, for of such is the kingdom of heaven. "O mother," said James, "how good the blessed Saviour was, to take *such little children* up, and bless them! I love the Saviour: my teacher says, if I pray to him he will give me a new heart, and then I shall wish to be good, therefore I shall be happy." This passage of Scripture was a subject on which he reflected for many days, and often spoke of the kindness of the Saviour, with a heart apparently full of love. Indeed, ever after that time, this passage was always a source of great pleasure to him. His prayers seemed more ardent, his sense of the presence and goodness of God, more constant, and his love to the Saviour was apparently much increased.

James also now exhibited more carefulness about his mother. When he observed she had a great deal of work to do, he would look about and if he thought of any way in which he could aid her he would do it of his own accord. He was a most careful observer of all the expressions of her countenance. If she appeared at all sad, or was not quite cheerful, James would say, "Mother, will you not let me stay with you and help you?" He was always grieved if his mother denied him this privilege.

Sometimes his mother, fearing he would suffer for want of exercise, would say, "Come James, go out now and play a while with the children." James always went as his mother directed, but when the boys did what he thought was wicked, he came into the house, and would often say, "O mother, I *cannot* stay with those children; they are so wicked."

One day his mother sent him away to play with the boys, just before she went out of the room. When she returned, she found James sitting in his chair, weeping. "Who has hurt you, my son?" said she, "No one, mother; but those boys are so wicked; *must* I stay with them?" So his mother allowed him to stay in the house.

CHAPTER V

When James was alone, he often amused himself by repeating some hymn which he had heard sung, or had learned in school. One of his favorites was,

> When I can read my title clear
>   To mansions in the skies,
> I'll bid farewell to every fear,
>   And wipe my weeping eyes.
>
> Should earth against my soul engage,
>   And fiery darts be hurled;
> Then I can smile at Satan's rage,
>   And face a frowning world.
>
> Let cares like a wild deluge come,
>   And storms of sorrow fall,
> May I but safely reach my home,
>   My God, my heaven, my all.
>
> There shall I bathe my weary soul
>   In seas of heavenly rest;
> And not a wave of trouble roll
>   Across my peaceful breast.[9]

Yes, my little reader; James thought of the mansions in the skies, which Christ told his disciples he was going to prepare,[10] and he prayed that he might be received there with all the good, and be happy. And now do you often think of that place, and remember that none but *good persons* can go there? will *you* not go away and pray that God would prepare you for that place?

James's attachment to his school will be seen to have been very strong, for when bad boys met him by the way, and said, "Come James, let us go and play," he would say, "No, I *am going to school.*" So he would hasten along as fast as he could, and leave *bad* boys behind to *play.* Sometimes he was attacked by these very wicked boys, and badly hurt, because he would not go with them. At other times they would call him a foolish little fellow for going to be shut up in the school room all day. When they had hurt him very badly, James would walk along slowly, so that he might dry up all the tears on his face, for he did not want to inform against them, because he had seen that it made his teacher unhappy. He has been often known to remain a long time by himself, until he could cease crying, for fear some one should inquire what was the matter, and then these bad boys who hurt him would be punished.

Perhaps you have seen some wicked boys who would pretend that they were badly hurt when they were not, so that they might cause others to be punished; but not so with James. He used to repeat the prayer, which says we must forgive those who have injured us.[11] Then he thought if he did not love and forgive boys who had done wrong to him, God would not be pleased with him. He had read how Christ our Saviour prayed for those who were crucifying him,[12] and how good Stephen prayed for those who were stoning him to death. Did you ever read about Stephen?[13] You will find the

account of his death in the 7th chapter of Acts beginning
with the 54th verse; you can ask your mother, or your teacher
about it next Sabbath.

James loved to pray, and seemed to engage in it with
proper feeling. His heart overflowed with gratitude to God
for the good that he bestowed upon him. In his seasons of
devotion he was regular, at least night and morning. Besides
these, he used sometimes to take the other children away and
pray with them, and talk with them about the blessed Saviour's dying for them,[14] and endeavor to persuade them to be
good and love the Lord. The little *preacher* was sometimes
very earnest in his exhortations. He seldom failed to gain the
attention of those who were about him at this season. The
opportunities which he sought, were when he could have a
room with the children. After an affectionate and earnest appeal to his little auditory, he would sometimes sing an appropriate hymn, and always closed with a prayer, for God's
blessing upon them. Persons of maturer years were surprised
at the appropriate and impressive addresses which he sometimes made. He often appeared to be filled with love for those
whom he addressed. When any thing was proposed for the
benefit of those who were suffering or without the gospel,
James used to pray to God to assist those who engaged in it.

One day while at school, his teacher told the children that
there were a great many thousands of their color who were
not allowed to read, who had no schools, nor any books.
These persons she said were slaves. The fathers and mothers
of a *great great* many children could not do as they pleased

with them, because other men said that they could sell them
or do what they pleased with them; they are called slaves.
These men did not want the slaves to know any thing about
reading the Bible. So they kept the children from school, and
while you are at school they make the slaves work very hard,
and because they don't know any thing at all about the word
of God they are sometimes very wicked. Then they are cru-
elly whipped. So they live and die without ever going to
school, or being taught by kind Sabbath school teachers.
"And now" said she, "will these children pray to God for the
little slave children and their parents?"

When James went home, he said to his mother, "Mother, I
have heard to-day about the poor slaves," and "my teacher
said, we might pray for them; now Ma, how shall I pray?"
"O James," said she, "your teacher has told you much about
them,—ask for them just what you think they need." After a
few moments of reflection James retired, and was heard to
offer the following simple prayer with much feeling. "O
Lord, pity the poor slaves, and let them be free, that they
may have their liberty, and be happy as I am,—and may they
have good teachers to learn them to read, as I have, and make
them all very good. Amen."

After this time, in all his prayers, he remembered the poor
slaves, and prayed for them. Some person who knew that he
prayed for slaves, asked him if he would continue to pray if
God should set them all at liberty. "Yes," said James, "I
would still pray for them, and thank Heaven because my
prayer was heard." James was not like the little girl, who

said, if she prayed that God would enable her to be a good girl, and recite her lessons, she would not study and try to get them. James's prayer for himself was, that God would enable him to *study diligently*, and think of his lesson, that he might say it well. I fear there are many who believe that God must influence men to be willing to give the captive slave his liberty, and his rights, who do not ask God as constantly as he did, that he would do it. We are taught to pray for men in all conditions.

You will see, if you look back to the short prayer of James, that he prayed that the poor slaves might be as *happy as he was*. This was doing as our blessed Saviour told those who loved him to do, when he said, You shall love your neighbor as yourself.[15] Will you remember and offer the same prayer for slaves and all in distress?

CHAPTER VI

About this time a Sabbath school was commenced near Mrs. Jackson's, in which James was entered as one of the pupils.[16] Here he was placed under the care of a new teacher, who soon discovered that he was a most interesting and attentive scholar. His attachment to the school was so strong, that neither cold nor rain would keep him from it, whenever his mother would permit him to attend. Here, in a small class, the teacher would impart instruction under more favorable circumstances than at a common school, and the interest which good children feel, will always be proportioned to the attention bestowed on them.

On the Sabbath morning, James would always inquire if he might go to Sabbath school to-day, and when allowed to go, he was always there in season to hear the prayer offered at the opening of the school.

When at home, he often spoke of the dear Sabbath school, and would try to make his mother more happy by repeating some little hymns which he had learned there.

At the week day school James was not only a good quiet boy, but he was an industrious scholar too. Whatever lesson his teacher directed his class to learn, he immediately commenced, and cheerfully continued to study, until he had entirely learned it. His memory was uncommonly good, because his attention to what he heard, or read in his book, was very careful. In discretion he excelled all, not only of his own age, but those who were many years older. After being in school five or six quarters he was always at the head of his class, though there were some boys in it twice his age. This quickness and diligence gained him much praise and commendation, but even under these circumstances James did not become proud and unkind to those who were not able to get a lesson so well as he could. His teacher has often seen him trying to help a boy who was *below him* in the class, and when he had learned him to spell or read, he seemed to be much pleased.

As all these excellent traits of character appeared, and strengthened, the attachment of his teacher could not fail to become stronger and stronger. She has often thought that the hours which she spent in teaching this dear child, were among the most happy of her life. His constant desire was to please her, while in the school; and, indeed, he often seemed to *anticipate* her wishes. In the government of the other children he was an assistant, by his example, and others were often referred to him as a pattern for their conduct.

His attachment to his mother strengthened with his mind and body, and as he was always in such fine health, she scarcely thought of his dying and leaving her. When with his mother alone, he would often repeat the passage about little children coming to Christ, and sometimes say, "Well, Ma, I want to go to him; I want to be blessed, and be good." At these times he would inquire about heaven, and his father, whom his mother had often told him about, and when she told him that all good persons would go there and be for ever happy, his eyes kindled with pleasure, for he seemed to feel that *there* was *his home.*

We must be indulged in saying, we never saw a child who seemed so much like innocence itself. The grace of God is to be magnified for what he was, for there can be *scarcely* a doubt but that he was under the special influence of his gracious Spirit. His overcoming temptation, his love for all persons, his forgiving temper towards all who had injured him, was not like the disposition which *children commonly* exhibit.

My dear reader, do you sometimes feel when some one wrongs you, that you *will repay him* for it, by doing something bad to him? That is wrong, and when you *feel* so, you are tempted. Now if you pray, "lead us not into temptation,"[17] you must *try, and try hard,* not to do that wrong which you feel you are *inclined* to do.

James was very fond of singing, and sometimes when he took the children to talk and pray with them, he would sing some of those little hymns which he had learned at school. His affectionate faithfulness toward children in his own family was an example for all who love God. After singing, he would tell the children of singing in heaven. There all will sing glory to God and the Lamb, for ever.

What I have said, shows that James remembered what he was told was in the word of God. His teacher among other things learned him the *commandments*,[18] and you know one of them tells us to keep the Sabbath day holy.[19] Now, James knew that God gave these commandments, and that he wanted every body to keep them.

His teacher told him how the great God wrote these commandments on flat pieces of stone, like a piece of board, and
gave them to Moses,[20] and he put them into a box, and kept
them there, except when they were read and taught to the
people, and the children;[21] then she told him, God wanted all
persons to obey these laws which he had made.

We have before said, that James remembered and obeyed
what was taught him. He thought much about this command,
for he saw a great many people who performed labour, or
were in the street, engaged in wicked or profane conversation. James knew this was the day on which the blessed Saviour rose from the dead, and he had been told that he used to
meet with his disciples on this day, and teach them and pray
with them;[22] so James thought he should be glad to keep the
holy Sabbath, just as the Lord would have him. A few Sab-
baths after James had learned this command, his mother put
some coffee into the coffee mill, and told him to grind it for
breakfast. James took the mill and began to turn, but soon he
almost stopt, and seemed thinking of something; his sister
seeing this, said, "Ma, shall I grind the coffee for you?" After
a moment, her mother said, "Yes, I guess you must; James is
lazy this morning." James looked mildly on his mother, a
tear glistening in his eye, (for he was grieved at the words of
reproach from his mother,) and said, "Ma, did I not split
wood for you yesterday?" "Yes, James, but that has nothing
to do with grinding the coffee *this morning*." "Well, Ma, is
not this the Sabbath?" "Yes." Then James said to his mother,
"The commandment says, Remember the Sabbath, to keep it

holy; and thou shalt *not do any* work in it;[23] and now, Ma, ought I to grind the coffee?" His mother was so much surprised at the thoughtful conscientiousness of the child that she hesitated for a moment, while James sat the mill down upon the floor. Then his mother said, "Well, James, you need not grind the coffee if you feel so about it." In a short time, James learned from his teacher, what was proper to be done on the Sabbath. So he was very careful not to do any work which was not necessary on that holy day.

I have related this anecdote, to show you how careful James was not to do what he thought *might be wrong*. I hope all who read this will remember the Sabbath, to keep it holy. Do you know the verse about the Sabbath? I will write it here, that you may learn it; and when you think of James and the coffee, you may repeat these words:

> I must not work,
> I must not play,
> Upon God's holy Sabbath day.[24]

Everybody who knew James, loved him; and he was often praised for his love of study, and obedience to his teachers. When people praised him, it did not make him proud and noisy, as I have seen some boys. But James always seemed to say, You should not praise a child to his face.

There was a manliness and propriety in all his conduct. When persons, who knew how easily he recollected what he heard, tried to learn him something foolish, he would not take any interest in it. He knew far better than is common, what was valuable and what was not. He forgot the foolish things that people tried to teach him, by *learning* what *was good*.

Those who used to see him do so much while he was so young, to make those about him happy, often thought that he would do a great deal of good when he became a man. His mother often pleased herself with thinking how happy she should be when her little James became a man. She thought he would love to do good, and teach others to love God. He was much engaged in his school, and every day he became more and more attached to his books and his teacher. She too saw every day more of his lovely disposition, and daily received increasing pleasure from discovering an increasing strength of intellectual power.

CHAPTER VII

James had often heard his teacher tell of persons who were sick and in distress. She told them too that all must die; and when we die, those who loved God and were good would go to heaven, and those who were bad would be sent away from the blessed Saviour forever. On these themes James delighted to dwell in his thoughts. He believed he loved the Saviour. O, said James, the blessed Saviour did receive children; and when I die, I shall go to be where he is. So he said of his teacher,

> I love to hear her talk of death,
>> And tell me to prepare
> To give to God my fleeting breath,
>> And go where angels are.

On Monday morning, the 28th Oct. 1833, he went to school apparently as well as usual; at noon he went home, and in the afternoon returned again to school, and read with his class; but soon after, as he was coming up to his teacher he fainted, and fell on the floor. He was taken up, and as soon as help could be procured he was carried home.

His mother sent for a physician immediately. When he came, he ordered some medicine, and directed his mother to have his feet bathed in warm water. After a short time he revived, and when he could speak aloud, he exclaimed, "Glory, honour, praise, and power, be unto the Lamb for ever and ever."[25] Perhaps at this time he was not fully sensible what he said, but his mind was on God. After some little time he relapsed into a state of insensibility, and soon after he was seized with violent convulsions, which continued all night with but short intervals. His distress was very great. His limbs were drawn into almost every possible position. He could not speak during all this great distress.

In the morning he appeared much exhausted, but after a little time recovered some strength, and was quite cheerful. He made no complaint of the pain that he suffered. His fever had raged to such a degree that his thirst was great, and he often called for water. After continuing quite calm for some time, at length he called his mother to his bed side. When she came, he requested her to send for his teacher. She had been with him during the night, but he was in such distress that he did not appear conscious of it.

His mother sent for her; but before she entered the room, another lady went to his bed to see if he would know her. She said to him, "Whom do you want, James?" "My teacher," said he, and added, "you are not her."

His teacher soon entered the room, and as she approached the bed she said, "Do you know *me*, James?" "Yes," said he emphatically, "I hope I *know my teacher.*"

His teacher said, "You are very sick, James."

James said, "Yes, I am sick."

Teach. "I hope you will soon be better, and before long go to school again."

James. "No; I do not want to get well, I would rather die;

for then I shall go and be with God, and the blessed Saviour."

Teach. "Are you willing, James, to leave the school, and your teacher, and your mother?" After a moment's thought, James said "Yes, I am willing to die; for then I shall go to the blessed Saviour, and I want to be with him, for he said, Suffer little children to come to me, and forbid them not, for of such is the kingdom of heaven." He then commenced singing a hymn, which he had learned at school, which described the Saviour blessing the little children whom he had called to him.[26]

After singing this, he remained silent a few moments, with his eyes apparently fixed on something above him.

He seemed to feel very deeply, for he raised his hand toward heaven and said, "O God, that was *my dear* Saviour who said that. I want to go away and be with him. O, I want to go away from this wicked world, and live always with the blessed Saviour in heaven. There is nothing wicked there."

His mind now appeared calm; and he laid quietly on the bed, while his thoughts seemed to be far away. Young as he was, we must suppose that he had employed more time in thinking of *his home in the skies,* than most children who had lived many times as long as he had. Yes, my dear reader, now, while James was on a sick bed, he looked to heaven as his home. Do you suppose that you could be so calm and happy, if you thought you were going to die? O, if you would be happy when God sends sickness upon you, you must be good, as little James was.

James now appeared to be engaged in prayer for some time. At intervals his countenance beamed with delight, while his soul seemed filled with love to his Saviour; he forgot all his pain, and suffering; he uttered no complaint, but readily took whatever the physician ordered. While in health, James had always been deeply affected, when he was told of the sufferings of the blessed Saviour, and his mind seemed now fixed in contemplation of those sufferings, so that his own were forgotten.

In the evening, the Rev. Mr. Snowden called to see James.[27] When he came to the bed where James was lying, he said, "Well, my child, you are very sick." "Yes sir," said James, "but God has carried me through another day, and he will soon take me to heaven."

Mr. S. said, "And with whom will you be there, James?" James replied, "With God and the blessed Saviour, and all who have been good in this world." James said much of heaven, and what glory and joy would fill the place; his heart was filled with delight, and his confidence in the Saviour was very strong. He often broke out in such expressions as these: "O, how good the Saviour was to think of such little children; and beside he *took* them and *blessed* them.[28] O, he is *my* Saviour, my own dear Saviour."

While James was speaking in this manner, Mr. Snowden said to some persons who were present, "What would an Infidel say if he heard these things." James heard it, and replied, "He would say, it was *God* who had done this."

His patience was wonderful; for during all his suffering

there was not the least fretfulness, or impatience, or any groaning or complaint about any thing.

The repeated convulsions which he had suffered, had made his flesh exceedingly sore, so that any movement caused him great pain. But notwithstanding all this, the only words of complaint which were heard, was once when his mother moved his hand to place it in a different position. While she had hold of it, James said, "O dear." But in a moment, he seemed very sorry.

His mother sat down by the bed, and asked him, "If he loved God now?" "Yes," said James, "I do love him." "Are you willing to die, and leave me and your brothers and sisters?"

At the mention of his brothers and sisters, a new thought seemed to come into his mind, and he said, "O Ma, I wish they all loved God and the blessed Saviour; yes, all of them may come to him, for he said, *Suffer little* children to come to me; his disciples did not want them to come; but *he* did take them and bless them.[29] And now I am going away to be with him, in those mansions in heaven which he has gone to prepare.[30] O, how glorious it will be, to be a saint in heaven—to be holy, and not to be with the wicked people: O, praise the Lord for this blessed Saviour. I pray, that all the dear children in the school, and in the Sabbath school, may be blessed of this dear Saviour, that they may be good and happy, and that they may go to heaven. This is my Saviour; he will carry me through death, and take me home."

The effort that he had made during this conversation exhausted him very much. His suffering increased to a great degree; so that it was thought by all he could not live but a short time. James seemed quite sensible that he should soon die. When his pain had subsided, and his strength a little returned, he called his mother to his bed, and said to her, "My dear mother, I love you very much; but I shall not stay with you much longer. I shall die, and go away to the blessed Saviour; if it is the will of God, I pray that he would spare me until to-morrow." Why he expressed this desire was never known; perhaps he thought he should have more strength to speak to those around him.

His strength was greatly diminished by his severe pain, and exertion in talking; so that for some time he remained silent, and seemed in great distress; for sometimes a half suppressed groan would escape him, in spite of all his efforts.

While he was in this state, the physician came in, and after remaining a few moments by his bedside, he went to another part of the room, where James could not see him. James asked his mother if the doctor had gone; when he was told he had not, "Well," said he, "I want to see him." The doctor came to the bedside, and said, "What do you want, James?" He replied, "I want to know if you *love God, my Saviour.*" "What did you say, James;" said the doctor. James repeated, with as much strength as he could, "Do you know God my Saviour?" The doctor was filled with surprise, and as he turned his face from the little sufferer, he exclaimed, *"That is a happy child;"* while James said, "He called little children to him and blessed them."[31]

While James was suffering so much, his strength wasted rapidly, and the hand of *death* seemed already on him. As his friends were standing around him, he asked them to sing a hymn, beginning thus:

> My Father has gone to heaven,
> O, how I long to be there too.

James joined in singing, and appeared very happy. Mr. Snowden was present, and offered a prayer. James still looked as if his heart was full of joy; but his eyes began to grow dim, his hands were cold, and in a few moments all was calm; the glazed eyes of this dear child once more beamed forth with unspeakable delight, and he exclaimed, "This is God my Saviour; O Lord, this is Jesus."——His eyes closed, his heart ceased to beat, and all was still. James was dead. Nothing remained but a cold and lifeless lump of clay. But his spirit, with which he used to love God, was carried away by angels to heaven. Yes, my dear reader, James died as quietly as you sometimes go to sleep. He was not afraid of death, for he loved the Saviour, and we believe he has gone to sing praises to the blessed Saviour for ever in heaven.

Now you have read all I have to say about James: you see how obediently he lived, and how happily he died. What do you remember particularly that you have read about him in this book?

Do you wish to be happy? Then you must be good; and you can't be good without trying, and sometimes trying very hard too. Do you think it was easy for James to be kind to boys who were unkind to him? If it was, then it may be easy for you.

You see James loved his mother so much that he always obeyed her; and when he did not know what was right, he asked her about it, and did just as *she thought* was right, and *not as bad children* told him to do.

He loved to hear the Bible read; and when it told what people should, or what they should not do, he remembered it, and prayed to God that he would help him keep these things in his mind, and make him love to do them. He kept away from wicked children, and prayed for them. Finally, he did as well as he knew how to do.

Now do you remember the words written in large letters which he used to think of so often? I will write them again here, so that you can find them easily when you want to look at them. Here they are:

THOU, GOD, SEEST ME!

LOVE YOUR ENEMIES;—AND

DO TO OTHERS AS YOU WISH OTHERS TO DO TO YOU.[32]

If you remember the first line, which I have written in large letters, you will not be inclined to do what you are forbidden to do by your parents, if they *are* out of your sight.

When you think of the second, you will not be inclined to injure those who have done wrong to you.

And if you always recollect the last, you will not injure any person who is poor, or in distress, or colored.

All who read this book, if they do not love God must have

a new heart. Will not all pray to God that their hearts may be changed; so that when they die, they may feel sure that they shall go to be with the blessed Saviour *for ever,* where they may join with James, and sing glory to God and the Lamb, and when a thousand years are ended, then the song will be sweet as ever, and all the good angels will join in singing this song of praise to God and the Lamb:

> Ten thousand thousand are their tongues,
> But all their joys are one.[33]

"THE LITTLE BLIND BOY"

There was a little boy of a dark skin, who was so blind that he could not see any thing at all; and there was a school where they taught poor blind children to read, and to do a great many kinds of work.[34] So the child asked his mother, if those good people would not take him in among the rest, and learn him. After some time, she went and asked the people who were at that institution, if they would take her little blind boy. The lad was delighted, and longed for his mother to return. But when she came back, she was very much grieved, for she had to tell the poor little boy, that the men who had the charge of the institution did not think best to have him come to their school.

Some one who loves little children heard about this, and wrote the following piece of poetry:—

THE LITTLE BLIND BOY

Mother, dear mother, do let me go!
You promised last week that I should, you know,
When you told me how happy the blind boys are,
How they sport and play, and are free from care;
How they learn with their finger ends to read,
And go every where with no one to lead,
And sing like a bird from its tight cage freed—
   Mother, do let me go!

They pity the blind boy, they weep for his wo—
I would, my son, but the men say, NO!
And love to give, (if his skin is white,)
To his darkened mind, truth's holy light;
But how can they see through your sooty skin,
To be perfectly sure there's a soul within?
And to teach a brute—why, 'twould be a sin—
    So the kind hearted men say, NO!

But mother, I *know* I've got a soul!
It burns in my breast like a living coal—
It restlessly struggles, and pants to leap out
From its prison so dreary to wander about:
Let me go to the men, for although they can't see
My soul through my skin, yet they *can set it free!*
Oh, when I can read, how delightful 't will be—
    But how gloomy 't is now!

My son, it would do you no good to go—
I begged them with tears—but they answered, "NO;
For how can the children whose skins are white,
In their studies and sports with a black boy unite?
They would hate him so much that they could not stay?
It would break up their work and spoil their play,
And their parents would come and take them away."
    So 't will do no good to go.

But how will they *know* I am not white?
Can they learn, (as they do to read and write,)

By their finger ends? And, mother, did they
Who gave them their houses and money e'er say,
That a black outside was good reason why
A blind boy's mind in darkness should lie?
Did they do what they ought for the *soul* that can't die?
   Or thought they alone of the *skin?*

I would tell you, my child, had I ever been taught;
The same questions I asked, but they answered them not;
They told me—and scornfully bade me go back—
"They'd have nothing to do with a boy that was *black*."
But though life's richest blessings you ne'er can enjoy,
And still must remain a blind negro boy,
Be contented, my son, for 't is certainly true,
That MANY WITH EYES ARE FAR BLINDER THAN YOU.

"AM I TO BLAME?"

The following is about a little boy who was grieved because other boys shunned his company. See what he asks his mother in the last verse. What do you think of the question? The Bible says that God made of one blood all nations, to dwell upon the face of the earth;[35] and, also, that God is no respecter of persons;[36] and the reason is, because he looks on the *heart;* and you should look at the *conduct,* not the *skin.*

AM I TO BLAME?

"Mother, why do the boys turn out,
 Whene'er I pass them by?
They'll scarcely speak a word to me—
 This makes me often cry.

Sometimes I ask them if they will
 Unite with me in play;
But oh! they give me such a look,
 I'm forced to run away.

And if they have a pretty book,
 Which I should like to see,
They tell me it was never made
 For little boys like me.

Now tell me, mother, why it is
 That people slight me so:

I really think they do me wrong;
   Pray tell me if you know."

"'T is this, my child;—your Maker gave
   To you a darker skin;
And people seem to think that such
   Can have no mind within."

"Am I to blame? It cannot be:
   What God has done is right;
And he must be displeased with those
   Who little black boys slight."

Chronology

Articles and Letters

Notes

Chronology

1806   The Reverend Thomas Paul is installed as minister of the African Church, on Belknap Street. It is Boston's first African American church and the first black Baptist church established in the North.

1809   Susan is born in Boston to the Reverend Paul and his wife, Catherine Waterhouse Paul, of Cambridge.

1813   Harriet Jacobs, author of *Incidents in the Life of a Slave Girl*, is born in Edenton, North Carolina.

1823   Reverend Thomas Paul travels to Haiti under the auspices of the Massachusetts Baptist Home Missionary Society. His lack of French hinders his effectiveness, and he soon returns home.

1824   Catherine Paul assumes directorship of African School Number 2 and moves the classrooms into the family's home on George Street.

1826   Susan's father presides over the marriage of Maria Miller and James Stewart.

1827/   Harriet Wilson, author of *Our Nig*, is born in Milford,
1828   New Hampshire.

         Freedom's Journal, the first African American newspaper, begins publication in New York City.

1829   George Horton, a slave of the president of the University of North Carolina, publishes *The Hope of Liberty*, a volume of poems whose sale he hopes will raise enough money to buy his freedom.

David Walker, a Bostonian and a parishioner of the Reverend Samuel Snowden's May Street Church, publishes *Walker's Appeal, in Four Articles; Together with a Preamble, to the Colored Citizens of the World, But in Particular, and Very Expressly, to Those of the United States of America.*

1831   Thomas Paul dies of consumption and is eulogized as a man "loved and respected" by "all good people."

William Lloyd Garrison begins publishing *The Liberator,* a weekly antislavery newspaper based in Boston.

Bostonian Maria Stewart makes her debut as a public speaker and becomes the first American woman to speak to a mixed audience.

The History of Mary Prince, a West Indian Slave Related by Herself, with a Supplement by the Editor, to Which is Added the Narrative of Asa-Asa, a Captured African, is published.

Nat Turner's revolt occurs in Southampton, Virginia.

1832   Susan Paul forms the Juvenile Choir, a group made up of her primary school students. The choir performs a number of public concerts and makes special appearances at antislavery society meetings throughout New England.

1833   April: Paul is elected secretary of the newly formed African American Ladies' Temperance Society.

August: Paul pays fifteen dollars for a life membership in the New England Anti-Slavery Society.

October: James Jackson Jr. dies in Boston.

The American Anti-Slavery Society is founded.

The Boston Female Anti-Slavery Society (BFASS) is founded.

Lydia Maria Child publishes *An Appeal in Favor of That Class of Americans Called Africans.*

1834   March: Paul and the Juvenile Choir perform at the Salem Anti-Slavery Society meeting. In *The Liberator* William Lloyd Garrison documents the group's encounter with racist Boston coachmen who deny them transportation to the meeting.

April: Paul is one of the first African American women invited to join the BFASS and is appointed to the office of counselor.

June: Paul's older sister, Anne Catherine Paul Smith, dies. Susan assumes responsibility for her sister's four young children.

July: Paul and the Juvenile Choir perform at New England Anti-Slavery Society Independence Day services in Boston.

1835   January: Paul and the Juvenile Choir perform hymns during the opening ceremonies of the third annual meeting of the New England Anti-Slavery Society in Boston.

June: The first excerpt from the *Memoir of James Jackson* is published in *The Liberator.*

August: The second excerpt from the *Memoir* is published in *The Liberator.*

Maria Stewart's *Productions of Mrs. Maria Stewart* is published in Boston.

1836   *The Life and Religious Experiences of Jarena Lee, a Coloured Lady,* is published.

1837   May: Paul is one of two Boston delegates to attend the Anti-Slavery Convention of American Women in New York City.

Olaudah Equiano's *Olaudah Equiano or Gustavus Vassa, an Autobiography of a Negro,* is published.

1838   May: Paul attends the second Anti-Slavery Convention of American Women in Philadelphia and is elected one of the organization's vice presidents.

Charles Remond of Salem becomes the first African American lecturer for the New England Anti-Slavery Society.

1840   Members of the BFASS elect Susan Paul and Lydia Maria Child as two of their delegates to the annual meeting of the American Anti-Slavery Society.

1841   April: Susan Paul dies of consumption and is buried in St. Paul's Cemetery, in Boston. Her obituary notice is published in leading African American and antislavery newspapers such as the *Colored American, The Liberator,* and the *National Anti-Slavery Standard.*

Thomas Paul Jr. graduates from Dartmouth College and begins a teaching career.

Frederick Douglass makes his first antislavery speech in Nantucket, Massachusetts.

Articles and Letters

Article on a Performance by Susan Paul's Juvenile Choir, *The Liberator*, March 29, 1834

Never were our hopes of the speedy triumph of the anti-slavery cause throughout New England more sanguine—never were our own feelings more exhilarated—never have we witnessed a more interesting spectacle—than on Monday evening last. Invitations were given by the Salem Anti-Slavery Society (which has now more than 300 members) to Professor Follen of Cambridge, Rev. E. M. P. Wells of South Boston, Rev. Mr. Phelps, and Samuel E. Sewall, Esq. of this city, and to other gentlemen to attend a public meeting in the Second Baptist meeting house in that town and address the people on the great subject of emancipation.[1] They all complied with the invitation, and were greeted not only cordially but enthusiastically by an overflowing house. We have nothing to regret but our inability to give a report of their speeches in the present number of the *Liberator;* but the basis of each may be seen by the resolutions which were offered and unanimously adopted on that most interesting occasion—viz.

On motion of the Rev. Mr. Phelps,

Resolved, That the treatment of the slaves in the United States is such as to demand the sympathy of all men, and such as ought immediately be abandoned.

On motion of Mr. Garrison,

Resolved, That the best interests of the slaveholders will be secured and promoted by the immediate emancipation of their slaves.

On motion of Samuel E. Sewall, Esq.

Resolved, That the people of the United States, as a nation, tolerate and encourage slavery, and are involved in the guilt of slaveholding.

[We have not received a copy of the resolution offered by the Rev. Mr. Wells, and seconded by Professor Follen. A sketch of the late gentleman's remarks will appear in our next number.]

The meeting was opened by prayer by the Rev. Mr. Grew, of this city.[2] The Rev. Mr. Grosvenor presided over it with dignity and spirit, and made some brief but pertinent observations.[3] Additional interest was imparted to its proceedings by the presence and performances of a number of colored children, under the direction of Miss Susan Paul, from Boston, who were invited to attend, and sing a number of hymns selected for the occasion. The vast concourse of spectators expressed their gratification in repeated bursts of applause. Our Salem friends will remember that particular instances of the vulgar and criminal prejudices, which reign in New England against a colored complexion, were cited by some of the speakers—to which another might have been added, not known at that moment, the disclosure of which would have excited their strongest indignation. These coaches were engaged to carry Miss Paul and her juvenile choir to Salem;

these were driven up to her door at the hour specified in the bargain, but as soon as the drivers discovered that the children were somewhat darker in complexion than themselves, they got into a rage, and profanely declared that "they would be d——d if they were to carry a load of *niggers* in the best coaches in Boston—they would sooner have their throats cut from ear to ear"!!! So these highly polished, intelligent *gentlemen* indignantly mounted their seats, cracked their whips, and drove back to their appropriate home—the stable—having violated their contract, and exhibited a meanness of conduct which places them far beneath the lowest slave in the republic.

In point of refinement, intelligence, and moral worth, the inhabitants of Salem have no superior, and nobly are they combining all these great qualities to save our country from the disgrace and the curse of slavery.

Letter from Susan Paul to William Lloyd Garrison, Published in *The Liberator*, April 5, 1834

We insert the following neatly written note from Miss Paul with much pleasure.

To the Editor of the Liberator:

Dear Sir—Seeing a notice in the last Liberator of the uncivil treatment we received from the drivers of the coaches provided to carry us to Salem, I thought it might be gratifying to our friends to know that others were afterwards procured, who were very accommodating. We were not surprised at

To the Editor of the Liberator.

Dear Sir— Seeing a notice in the last Liberator of the uncivil treatment we received from the drivers of the coaches provided to carry us to Salem, I thought it might be gratifying to our friends to know that others were afterwards procured, who were very accommodating. We were not surprised at our treatment from these persons, when we were informed that they agreed to attend the funeral of a very respectable person, a short time since, and on finding that the deceased was colored, they promptly refused! This is but a faint picture of that spirit which persecutes us on account of our color — that cruel prejudice which deprives us of every privilege whereby we might elevate ourselves — and then absurdly condemns us because we are not more refined and intelligent.

But this is no time to despair. The rapid progress of the cause you so successfully advocate will, ere long, annihilate the present corrupt state of things, and substitute liberty and its concomitant blessings.

We feel happy to express our gratitude publickly to our friends in Salem, for the very kind reception we received from them.

A sumptuous entertainment was provided for the children at the residence of Mr. Remond, and each member of the family did all in their power to contribute to our happiness; for which they will please to accept our thanks. We had many and urgent invitations from ladies and gentlemen to remain at their houses for the night, to whom, until being introduced on that evening, we were entire strangers. The Rev. Mr. Grosvenor, also, is deserving of our sincerest thanks for his earnest exertions in our behalf. Many a friend of the oppressed will be raised up through his instrumentality, and many a prayer will be offered to heaven, for the choicest blessings to rest upon him.

S. Paul.

Boston, April 1, 1834.

our treatment from these persons, when we were informed that they agreed to attend the funeral of a very respectable person, a short time since, and on finding that the deceased was colored, they promptly refused! This is but a faint picture of that spirit which persecutes us on account of our color —that cruel prejudice which deprives us of every privilege whereby we might elevate ourselves—and then absurdly condemns us because we are not more refined and intelligent.

But this is no time to despair. The rapid progress of the cause which you so successfully advocate will, ere long, annihilate the present corrupt state of things, and substitute liberty and its concomitant blessings.

We feel happy to express our gratitude publicly to our friends in Salem, for the very kind reception we received from them.

A sumptuous entertainment was provided for the children at the residence of Mr. Remond, and each member of the family did all in their power to contribute to our happiness, for which they will please to accept our thanks.[4] We had many and urgent invitations from ladies and gentlemen to remain at their houses for the night, to whom, until being introduced on that evening, we were entire strangers. The Rev. Mr. Grosvenor, also, is deserving of our sincerest thanks for his earnest exertions in our behalf. Many a friend of the oppressed will be raised up through his instrumentality, and many a prayer will be offered to heaven for the choicest blessings to rest upon him.

S. Paul

Boston, April 1, 1834

Letters from Students of the Union Evangelical
Sabbath School of Amesbury and Salisbury to the
Children of Susan Paul's School, and from Susan Paul
in Reply, Published in *The Liberator*, August 13, 1836

We invite attention to the interesting correspondence given
below, between the children of the Amesbury and Salisbury
Sabbath School, and those of Miss Paul's in this city.[5] If the
same lovely spirit which dictated this correspondence, were
cherished by all the children of all the Sabbath and Primary
schools in our land, the hateful prejudice which now grinds
the colored man in the dust, would expire long before the
present adult generation have left the stage. The example of
the children would shame their parents out of it, if it could
not be eradicated in any other way. The children of the
Amesbury and Salisbury Sabbath School will derive far
sweeter satisfaction from the recollection of this act of self-
denial, in devoting their holiday pocket money to the mental
and moral improvement of their indigent colored brothers
and sisters, than they would have done in spending ten-fold
the sum, for their own selfish gratification.

CORRESPONDENCE

Amesbury & Salisbury,
July 4, 1836
To the colored children of Miss Paul's school, Boston:
  Dear Friends,—We have heard about you and your
teacher lately, and we feel very much pleased to think that so
many colored children are under the care of a kind teacher,

who learns you to be wise and good. We remember to-day, as the bible tells us, those who are "in bonds," and we feel very sorry that there are so many children in our country, who have no kind teachers as you and as we have, but are obliged to live and die ignorant slaves. Oh, we *will* pity them, and we know that you *do*.[6]

Wicked men tell us that black children have no souls. But we know that you have souls—and we are very glad to hear that your souls are growing and filling up with wisdom and goodness, under the instruction of a kind teacher. You love her very much we know you must—and delight to please her.

Our parents always give us money when the 4th of July comes, to buy candy, &c. But we have concluded that it will be much better to-day, to send this money to your teacher, for your benefit. We do this to show our respect for you and your teacher, and the interest we feel in your welfare. We hope that you will grow up to be very wise and good people, and so put to shame those wicked men who say that colored people have no souls.

Let us all hope that not many more "independent days" will come, before every little girl and boy, white or black, in America, will be as free and as happy as we are.

Our love to you all,

The scholars of the Union Evangelical Sabbath School of Amesbury and Salisbury,—by their Superintendant,

A. MORRILL.[7]

P. S. We should like to receive a letter from you, directed to our superintendant.

Miss Paul:—The sum enclosed is three dollars. It is but a mite; yet as money saved by children out of their holiday pocket money, by the practice of a little self-denial, we trust you will deem it worthy of acceptance. A. M.

July 20, 1836
To the children of the Union Evangelical Sabbath School of Amesbury and Salisbury:

Dear Friends,—We have received your kind letter to us, and the money enclosed in it. We do not know how to express our thanks to you for this act of love. It has made us very glad to know that you think of us, and of the dear little children who are slaves.—We know of some little children who do not love us because we are colored; but we pity them and pray for them, for the blessed Saviour has told us in his word, to love our enemies.[8]

We have several school-mates who have been slaves, and we try to make them as happy as we can. We wish you could see how they try to learn, and how much they love our teacher. We should be glad if *all* the little slaves were in our school.

We know that you have a very good teacher, to let you send us such a pretty letter. It is the first one that we ever received, and we want to tell you how much good has been done with the money you sent in it. We all agreed that it should be spent for those children in the school who were most destitute, and our teacher has bought books and other necessary things with it, and we are very happy about it.

We hope you will come and see us when you visit Boston, for we love you very much, although we never saw you. We know that you are friends to us, because you have done so much for us. When you come to see us, we will sing to you about the slaves, and the Sabbath Schools, and about drinking rum.[9]

We wish all the children who attend Sabbath Schools felt as *you* do towards the poor and despised. Let us learn as fast as we can, and do all in our power to please our teachers. You will be happy to hear that we have a Temperance Society—and on the "fourth of July" we had a meeting.[10] Our Superintendant and others told us some interesting things, and some new members joined the Society, and we were much happier than we should have been if we had spent all the day in the streets.

We hope to hear from you again when it is convenient. Accept our love.

The children of Primary School, No. 6. Boston, by their teacher, SUSAN PAUL.

Mr. Morrill,—

Sir:—Please to accept my thanks for the interesting letter from your scholars to the children under my care, sent by you—also the very generous donation which it contained. You will be gratified to know that it was expended for the actual wants of some of the children. This act of kindness will ever be remembered with gratitude.

Respectfully, S. Paul.

Report on "Miss Paul's Juvenile Concert," *New York Evangelist*, February 25, 1837

From Our New-England Correspondent.

Boston, Feb. 11, 1837.

Dear Brother Leavitt[11]—I cannot tell when I have been more delighted, than I was on Thursday evening last, in attending Miss Paul's Juvenile Concert of colored children.[12] Miss Paul is the daughter of the late Rev. Mr. Paul, pastor of the African Baptist church. She teaches a primary school for colored children. Though tinged with the "hated stain," she is evidently a superior woman. The pieces performed were selected with much taste and skill; and she manifested throughout, the most perfect self-possession, united with great modesty and propriety of conduct. She was able also to keep the most perfect command of the children. They were about fifty in number; and I have never seen so many children together, for so long a time, (more than two hours,) with greater propriety of behavior; nor did I ever witness a more interesting group assembled on any occasion. Their eyes sparkled with sprightliness, and their countenances beamed with intelligence. But the sweetness and melody of their voices is incomparable. If I could report the singing, I would promise your readers a most delightful repast. In the selection and arrangement of the pieces, there was an agreeable intermingling of the pastoral, playful, pathetic, and serious; but nothing in the least degree objectionable.

But what astonished and delighted me most of all, was the performances of several very little girls, one of whom, I think, could not have been more than three or four years old. She sung all the pieces, with apparent ease, and pronounced the words with distinctness and propriety. She even sung several *solos*, with her single voice, with clearness and propriety. The following little piece created great amusement. She stood up alone, and sung,

> I am a cuckoo, my name is Cuckoo,
> The children call me Cuckoo,
> And should you ever forget my name,
> I'll always tell you, Cuckoo.
> When winter comes, the woods are my home,
> In summer I sing in the meadows,
> Thus lives the cuckoo, his mate the cuckoo,
> And all the little cuckoos.[13]

I could not have believed that a child of her age could be trained to sing independently with so much correctness and propriety. One of the boys, also, who sung several *solos*, has the most melodious voice I ever heard. No instrument of music will compare with it.

Several of the pieces produced no small emotion, from their bearing upon a certain "delicate subject," coming as

they did from those who must *feel* their meaning. As I do
not recollect having seen them before, I will copy the following:

> Hark to the clank! What means that sound?
> 'Tis slavery shakes its chain!
> Man driving man, in fetters bound—
> And this where freedom reigns!
> Say, what have these poor wretches done,
> That chains their lot should be?
> Are they not punished to atone
> For some great robbery?
> Or black atrocious homicide?
> Or treasonable plan?
> Ah no! To pamper human pride,
> Man chains his fellow man!
> Man's flesh and blood each day behold
> Like swine to market driven
> God's noblest creatures bought and sold
> By Christians! Heirs of heaven!
> Great God! does such hypocrisy
> Not call for vengeance due?
> Shall patriots shout for liberty,
> And act the tyrant too?
> They say by nature all are free,
> But blush when truth unfolds,
> To own how black the heart must be,
> Who lives by trading souls.[14]

Another, commencing "Ye who in bondage pine," was deeply touching;[15] and another, "Sons of Columbia! awake from your sleeping," produced a thrilling effect.[16] But the following, sung by those whom the Colonization Society would send to Africa, with their own consent, is the most pointed and conclusive, as well as touching argument against that scheme, that I ever heard.

THIS, THIS IS OUR HOME

Great God, if the humble and weak are as dear
To thy love as the proud, to the children give ear!
Our brethren would drive us in deserts to roam;
Forgive them, O Father, and keep us at home,
     Home, sweet home!
We know of no other; this, this is our home.

Here, here our loved mothers relaxed from their toils,
To watch o'er our cradles and joy in our smiles;
Here the bones of our fathers lie buried; and here
Are friends, wives, and children, ay, all we hold dear,
     Home, sweet home, &c.

Here is law, here is learning, and here we may move,
Most merciful God, in the light of thy love.
Boasts Afric such blessings? Oppressors, declare!
Oh no, we may seek, but shall not find them there,
     Home, sweet home, &c.

Columbia, dear land of our birthright! may He
Who made us a people, rain blessings on thee!

FROM THY BOSOM NO PLEADING SHALL TEMPT US TO ROAM;
Till force drive us from it, this, this is our home.
    Home, sweet home,
Till force drive us from it, this, this is our home.[17]

Many of the pieces were difficult; yet they were performed with such correctness and propriety, as to show that not only the teacher, but the children, must have some practical knowledge of the science of music. It could not be all imitation. The pronunciation was distinct, and as correct as will be heard in conversation, in any circle of refined society. I think such things well calculated to remove the unjust feeling that exists towards these people.

$\mathcal{N}otes$

1. Marilyn Richardson, *Maria Stewart: America's First Black Woman Political Writer, Essays and Speeches* (Bloomington: Indiana University Press, 1987), p. 3.

2. Nathaniel Paul (1786–1839) and his brother Benjamin (d. 1836) were highly regarded in the American and international abolitionist movements. Nathaniel was instrumental in founding several African American churches in the Northeast. From 1820 to 1830 he was the minister of the African Baptist Church, the only African American church in Albany, New York. In the 1830s Nathaniel spent four years in England, where he advocated abolition in the House of Commons, consulted with such influential British abolitionists as Thomas Clarkson, and lectured throughout the British Isles in order to raise funds for the newly established Negro settlement in Wilberforce, Ontario.

   Benjamin Paul, a minister in New York City from 1826 to 1830, was extremely active in community uplift programs and education. Like his brother Nathaniel, he was an advocate of African American emigration. In 1830 Benjamin Paul and his family joined and played a prominent role in the organization of the Wilberforce settlement in Upper Canada. His daughter was a teacher there, and his son Thomas served as principal of one of the settlement's two schools, an institution so highly regarded that it attracted white students from the surrounding area.

   For additional information about the Paul brothers, see the

entries devoted to them in Rayford Logan and Michael Winston, eds., *Dictionary of American Negro Biography* (New York: W. W. Norton, 1982).

3. The *Memoir* is cited in the entry for Susan Paul in Jean Fagan Yellin and Cynthia Bond, comps., *The Pen Is Ours: A Listing of Writings by and about African-American Women before 1910 with Secondary Bibliography to the Present* (New York: Oxford University Press, 1991). The only published summary is found in Paul Goodman's posthumous *Of One Blood: Abolitionism and the Origins of Racial Equality* (Berkeley: University of California Press, 1998). Elsewhere Paul is cited for her antislavery work rather than for her authorship of the *Memoir*.

4. Boston city directories for 1820–1823 and 1825–1826 contain the following listings for James Jackson Sr.: 1820: "Jackson, James, Washington Street"; 1821: "Jackson, James, labourer, Cambridge Street"; 1822: "Jackson, James, labourer, Vine"; 1823: "Jackson, James, labourer, Vine"; 1825: "Jackson, James, Butolph"; and 1826: "Jackson, James, Butolph" (*Boston City Directory* [Boston: John A. Frost and Charles Stimpson, 1820–1823, 1825–1826]; U.S. Bureau of the Census, *Fourth Census of the United States, 1820—Massachusetts, Suffolk County,* National Archives and Records Administration, Northeast Regional Branch, Pittsfield, Mass., microfilm reel 53, p. 147).

5. U.S. Bureau of the Census, *Fourth Census, 1820—Massachusetts,* microfilm reel 53, p. 147.

6. Despite the absence of death records for James Jackson Sr., it is clear that he died before 1830, the year of the next federal census. Boston city directories indicate that he died sometime after publication of the 1826 edition and before early December 1828. City directories for 1826–1834 contain no entries for any females with the surname Jackson.

7. The 1830 federal census contains an entry for a "Free Colored Family" in Boston whose head of household is named Anna Jackson. The family includes one female aged 36–55, a fact that suggests a match with the 1820 entry for James Jackson's wife, who was then between 26 and 45; one male under 10; eight males and one female aged 10–24; and one female aged 24–36. James Jackson Jr. could certainly be the child under 10; the sister mentioned in Paul's narrative could have been born shortly after the 1820 census and thus be aged 10. The eight males could be James's brothers, members of the extended family, or a combination of relatives and male boarders (U.S. Bureau of the Census, *Fifth Census of the United States, 1830—Massachusetts, Suffolk County*, microfilm reel 65, p. 61). Boston city directories, however, contain no entries for an African American woman named Anna Jackson. The 1835 directory does list a widow named Hannah Jackson living on West Centre Street near Southac, in the African American Beacon Hill neighborhood (*Stimpson's Boston Directory* [Boston: Charles Stimpson Jr., 1835], p. 392).

The 1840 Massachusetts census lists a "Free Colored Family" in Boston named Jackson with a female head of household named Fanny Jackson, aged 36–55, one female aged 24–36, and one male aged 10–24 (U.S. Bureau of the Census, *Sixth Census of the United States, 1840—Massachusetts, Suffolk County*, microfilm reel 97, p. 208). The 1840 city directory includes an entry for an African American woman named Fanny Jackson living on May Street, in the African American Beacon Hill neighborhood (*Stimpson's Boston Directory* [Boston: Charles Stimpson Jr., 1840], p. 448).

Because census returns did not include the names of dependents until 1860, it is not possible to match the returns and directory listings conclusively. The Jacksons' anonymity underscores their status as an ordinary American family for whom there is no detailed genealogical record in early censuses.

8. For the most comprehensive account of Thomas Paul's life, see J. Carleton Hayden, "Thomas Paul," in Logan and Winston, *Dictionary of American Negro Biography,* pp. 482–483. On Paul and Boston community politics, see George Levesque, "Inherent Reformers—Inherited Orthodoxy: Black Baptists in Boston, 1800–1873," *Journal of Negro History* 60 (October 1975): 491–519, and *Black Boston: African American Life and Culture in Urban America, 1750–1860* (New York: Garland, 1994). See also J. Marcus Mitchell, "The Paul Family," *Old Time New England* 63 (Winter 1975): 73–77.

9. Robert Hayden, *African Americans in Boston: More than 350 Years* (Boston: Trustees of the Public Library of the City of Boston, 1991), p. 129.

10. There are conflicting accounts about when the African Church was founded. Sharon Harley, *Timetables of African American History* (New York: Simon & Schuster, 1995), p. 70, gives the year 1805. In *African Americans in Boston,* Robert Hayden suggests that the church was established in 1806. In *Black Bostonians: Family Life and Community Struggle in the Antebellum North* (New York: Holmes & Meier, 1979), James and Lois Horton, basing their chronology on Boston Baptist Church records, report that the church and congregation were formally recognized in 1805 and that the meetinghouse itself was completed one year later.

11. Paul's Belknap Street Church and the Reverend Samuel Snowden's African Methodist Chapel were the two African

American churches established in Boston between 1805 and 1835. By 1841 Snowden's chapel had been renamed the May Street Methodist Episcopal Church. For more on African American antebellum church history and attendance patterns, see James Horton and Lois Horton, *In Hope of Liberty: Culture, Community, and Protest among Northern Free Blacks, 1700–1860* (New York: Oxford University Press, 1997); and Levesque, *Black Boston,* which includes data on church attendance, church-sponsored education and outreach, and ministerial activities.

12. Richardson, *Maria Stewart,* p. 3.

13. William Lloyd Garrison (1805–1879) was the founder and editor of Boston's antislavery newspaper, *The Liberator.* During the 1830s Garrison was instrumental in the campaign to organize the New England Anti-Slavery Society, founded in 1831 at the Reverend Thomas Paul's African Church, and the American Anti-Slavery Society in 1833. Garrison was also involved in numerous efforts to improve the quality of African American life and education. He was quite familiar with the Paul family. He toured England on an antislavery fundraising campaign with Susan's uncle, the Reverend Nathaniel Paul, sponsored Thomas Paul Jr.'s apprenticeship at the *Liberator* office, and supported Susan Paul's publication efforts and work in the primary schools, the Boston Female Anti-Slavery Society, and Juvenile Choir performances. For additional information see Oliver Johnson, *William Lloyd Garrison and His Times* (Boston: B. B. Russell, 1880); John Thomas, *The Liberator: William Lloyd Garrison* (Boston: Little, Brown, 1963); and Henry Mayer, *All On Fire: William Lloyd Garrison and the Abolition of Slavery* (New York: St. Martin's Press, 1998).

14. *The Liberator*, February 22, 1834, p. 30.

15. The lack of family papers and the loss of African Meeting House records to fire make it difficult to determine whether the Paul children were tutored privately or attended the segregated schools available to them. Most likely they received some instruction from their mother. If they attended the African school in their father's church, Susan and her siblings would have been taught by one or more of the African American teachers hired between 1808 and 1818: Cyrus Vassal (1808); Prince Sanders, future diplomatic officer for the Haitian emperor Christophe (1809–1812); Mr. Willey (1812); and Peter Tracy (1813–1818). On early African American schools in Boston, see Levesque, *Black Boston;* John Daniels, *In Freedom's Birthplace: A Study of the Boston Negroes* (Boston: Houghton Mifflin, 1914); and Arthur O. White, "Prince Saunders: An Instance of Social Mobility among Antebellum New England Blacks," *Journal of Negro History* 60 (October 1975): 526–535.

16. Arthur O. White, "The Black Leadership Class and Education in Antebellum Boston," *Journal of Negro Education* 42 (Fall 1973): 511. In 1833 Bascom's tenure at the African School ended after parents charged that he had made inappropriate advances toward young female students. The allegations against the school's second white male instructor were never investigated, but he was eventually transferred to another city school. On the instructors and history of the African School, see George Levesque, "Before Integration: The Forgotten Years of Jim Crow Education in Boston," *Journal of Negro Education* 48 (Fall 1979): 113–125.

17. Rev. George T. Chapman, *Sketches of the Alumni at Dartmouth College* (Cambridge, Mass.: Riverside Press, 1867), p. 321.

Thomas Paul Jr. may have attended the African Church school during teacher John B. Russwurm's tenure and been inspired by his impressive educational achievements. Russwurm, who taught in Boston between 1821 and 1824, later enrolled at Bowdoin College and became one of the nation's first African American college graduates. For more on Russwurm, see Clarence Contee's entry in Logan and Winston, *Dictionary of American Negro Biography*, pp. 538–539.

18. Boston School Committee member and historian Joseph Wightman reports that Boston's first public African American primary school for younger children opened in Reverend Thomas Paul's Belknap Street Church on August 7, 1822. The annual rent for the space was seventy-two dollars, and forty-seven students enrolled in the school, which was directed by a Miss Charlotte Foster. Apparently a grammar school was already housed in the church's basement. See Joseph Wightman, *Annals of the Boston Primary School Committee, from Its First Establishment in 1818, to Its Dissolution in 1855* (Boston: Geo. C. Rand & Avery, 1860), p. 69.

19. White, "Black Leadership Class," p. 511.

20. Wightman, *Annals of the Boston Primary School Committee*, p. 94.

21. Ibid., p. 95.

22. Horton and Horton, *In Hope of Liberty*, p. 120. For more on African Americans in nineteenth-century America, see Robert Cottrol, *The Afro-Yankees: Providence's Black Community in the Antebellum Era* (Westport, Conn.: Greenwood Press, 1982); Leonard Curry, *The Free Black in Urban America, 1800–1850* (Chicago: University of Chicago Press, 1981); Bert Loewenberg and Ruth Bogin, *Black Women in Nineteenth-Century*

American Life (University Park: Pennsylvania State University
Press, 1976); Gary Nash, *Forging Freedom: The Emancipation
Experience in the Northern Seaport Cities, 1775–1820* (Cam-
bridge, Mass.: Harvard University Press, 1988); and Harry
Reed, *Platform for Change: The Foundations of the Northern
Free Black Community, 1775–1865* (East Lansing: Michigan
State University Press, 1994).

23. In 1849 Thomas Jr. accepted an offer to return to Boston as
principal of the Smith School, the relocated and renamed primary school that he may have attended in his youth. Shortly
after his arrival he was thrust into the center of heated community and family debates about the future of segregated
schooling and school choice. The appointment was immediately controversial: his cousin Thomas Paul Smith supported
segregated schooling, and another cousin, five-year-old Sarah
Roberts, became the plaintiff in a suit brought against the city
of Boston by her father, an enterprising printer named Benjamin Roberts who was frustrated by his daughter's exclusion
from white schools close to their home. The Roberts case, presented by Boston attorneys Charles Sumner and Robert Morris, was heard before the Massachusetts Supreme Judicial
Court. The 1850 decision against Sarah Roberts established the
precedent for the 1896 *Plessy v. Ferguson* "separate but equal"
ruling, as well as the 1954 school desegregation suit, *Brown v.
Board of Education.* For a detailed account of the Roberts case,
see Horton and Horton, *Black Bostonians;* and contemporary
court transcripts and arguments in December 1849 issues of
The Liberator.

24. Boston's African American proprietors also sold tickets for
Paul's concerts. James Barbadoes, a prosperous barber and

clothier and one of the city's most prominent abolitionists, was, with James Loring and the *Liberator* office, a well-known source for concert tickets. He also advertised and sold anti-slavery books and pamphlets from his shop on Brattle Street.

25. *New York Evangelist,* February 25, 1837, p. 33; reprinted in George E. Carter and C. Peter Ripley, eds., *Black Abolitionist Papers* (Ann Arbor: University Microfilms International, 1984), reel 1:0958.

26. *New York Evangelist,* February 25, 1837, p. 33.

27. Anne Boylan, "Evangelical Womanhood in the Nineteenth Century: The Role of Women in Sunday Schools," in *History of Women in the United States,* ed. Nancy Cott, vol. 13: *Religion* (Munich: K. G. Saur, 1993), pp. 94–112; quotation p. 95.

28. On Philadelphia organizations, see Dorothy Sterling, ed., *We Are Your Sisters: Black Women in the Nineteenth Century* (New York: W. W. Norton, 1984), p. 104.

Accounts of Benjamin Paul's work in New York City were published regularly in *Freedom's Journal,* the first African American newspaper. During his four-year tenure as a minister in New York City, Paul worked closely with several black ministers and community leaders, including the Reverend Peter Williams; the Reverend Samuel E. Cornish, minister of the First Presbyterian church and editor of *Freedom's Journal;* and John Russwurm, former Boston African school instructor and coeditor of *Freedom's Journal.* Benjamin Paul served on advisory committees with his fellow black ministers and organized to promote and support the benevolent society work of black women. He endorsed the community's campaigns to establish schools for the city's African American youth, delivered keynote addresses at the opening of at least one African American school, and was frequently listed as a contact in advertisements for city tutors and private schools.

For more on women's involvement in African American benevolent organizations and other antebellum mutual-aid societies, see Horton and Horton, *In Hope of Liberty,* esp. chap. 6; Richard Brown, "The Emergence of Voluntary Associations in Massachusetts, 1760–1830," *Journal of Voluntary Action Research* 2 (April 1973): 64–73; and Daniel Perlman, "Organizations of the Free Negro in New York City, 1800–1860," *Journal of Negro History* 56 (July 1971): 181–197.

29. Reed, *Platform for Change,* p. 78.
30. Ibid., p. 76.
31. Hayden, *African Americans in Boston,* p. 19. For contemporary reports of the society's founding, Paul's election, and details about the other officers, see *The Liberator,* April 20, 1833.
32. William Lloyd Garrison to the Boston Female Anti-Slavery Society, April 9, 1834; Mary Grew to Garrison, April 11, 1834; both in Boston Female Anti-Slavery Society Papers, Massachusetts Historical Society, Boston. For contemporary notes about the BFASS, see the collections at the Schlesinger Library, Radcliffe College, and at the Massachusetts Historical Society. For a detailed history of this women's auxiliary of the predominantly male New England Anti-Slavery Society, see Debra Gold Hansen, *Strained Sisterhood: Gender and Class in the Boston Female Anti-Slavery Society* (Amherst: University of Massachusetts Press, 1993). See also Jean Fagan Yellin and John Van Horne, eds., *The Abolitionist Sisterhood: Women's Political Culture in Antebellum America* (Ithaca: Cornell University Press, 1994); and Clare Taylor, *Women of the Anti-Slavery Movement* (New York: St. Martin's Press, 1995). For a compre-

hensive study of African American women's leadership in and contributions to organizations such as the BFASS, see Shirley Yee, *Black Women Abolitionists: A Study in Activism, 1828–1860* (Knoxville: University of Tennessee Press, 1992).

33. This first published excerpt of the *Memoir* was followed just over a month later by a second, more informative article. The bibliography on the *Memoir* in Yellin and Bond, *The Pen Is Ours,* wrongly states that the August 1835 article was the first on Paul's book to appear in that newspaper.

34. Mayer, *All On Fire,* p. 203. See also contemporary accounts in newspapers such as *The Liberator, Boston Courier,* and *Boston Morning Post.*

35. The 1837 delegation consisted of Paul, society president Mary Parker, secretary Martha Ball, and Julia Williams, a former student of Prudence Crandall and a teacher in the African American school founded by BFASS member Martha Ball and her sister, Lucille. Debra Hansen quotes an illuminating letter from member Anne Weston to her sister Deborah about the delegates. According to Weston, Susan Paul was chosen "because she was a favourable specimen of the coloured race," and Julia Williams was nominated "because the coloured people regard her as one of themselves, a light in which they do *not* regard Susan Paul" (*Strained Sisterhood,* p. 19). Weston's comment sheds important light on Paul's status in the black community. Since both she and Williams were teachers in the community and Paul's long-standing work with the children both fostered and required trust with parents in the neighborhood, it is likely that Paul's family background and record of publication led her neighbors to consider her not "one of themselves," even though by the mid-1830s the family's elite

status in the community was more symbolic than real because of its increasingly straitened financial circumstances.

36. Benjamin Quarles, *Black Abolitionists* (New York: Oxford University Press, 1969), p. 2.

37. See Reed, *Platform for Change,* on African American women's pioneering roles in abolitionist movements. Reed's discussion of how women like Maria Stewart, Susan Paul, and the mother-daughter team of Margaretta and Harriet Forten negotiated conventional domestic expectations and their roles in the public sphere clarifies the realities that black women faced as they began to do public service.

38. References to Susan Paul's engagement and to her unnamed fiancé's death appear in her obituary in *The Liberator,* April 23, 1841.

39. According to Paul's BFASS colleague Sarah Southwick, her sickness was the direct result of racial prejudice; during a steamboat voyage to New York, she was denied access to the "ladies' cabin" and was forced to endure inclement weather on deck. Yee, *Black Woman Abolitionists,* p. 28.

40. *The Liberator,* April 23, 1841, p. 67.

41. *National Anti-Slavery Standard,* July 29, 1841, p. 199.

42. *Colored American,* May 8, 1841, p. 39.

43. The Smith School was named in honor of white Bostonian Abiel Smith, who bequeathed five thousand dollars to be used for African American education in the city. In his speech at the school's dedication, Judge William Minot stated that racial inequality was directly linked to African American educational deprivation. Minot encouraged black members of his audience to take advantage of the resources available to them but suggested that elevation and progress would not be attained

quickly. His speech offers useful insights into contemporary assessments of the black community's prerogatives and agenda for educational reform. See *Mr. Minot's address: delivered at the dedication of the Smith School House in Belknap Street, March 3, 1835, to which are added a few friendly suggestions to the colored people in Boston* (Boston: Webster and Southard, 1835).

44. Levesque, *Black Boston,* p. 170.

45. Ibid., pp. 57, 58. In 1835 145 students—73 boys and 72 girls— were enrolled at the Smith School. Enrollment peaked in 1840, at 263, but dropped sharply in 1845 to only 180. See Levesque, *Black Boston,* on the regular upheavals in matters relating to separate schools for African Americans. For comprehensive histories of antebellum Boston, see Horton and Horton, *Black Bostonians;* James Horton, "Generations of Protest: Black Families and Social Reform in Ante-Bellum Boston," *New England Quarterly* 49 (June 1976): 242–256; and Adelaide Cromwell, *The Other Brahmins: Boston's Black Upper Class, 1750–1950* (Fayetteville: University of Arkansas Press, 1994). On antebellum education, see Stanley Schultz, *The Culture Factor: Boston Public Schools, 1789–1860* (New York: Oxford University Press, 1973); Carl Kaestle and Maris Vinovskis, *Education and Social Change in Nineteenth-Century Massachusetts* (Cambridge: Cambridge University Press, 1980); and Levesque, *Black Boston.*

46. Levesque, *Black Boston,* p. 171. As teachers and school administrators, Catherine Paul and her daughters Susan and Anne offered students and parents significant educational stability. They conducted African School Number 2 in their George Street home uninterruptedly from 1824 to 1837.

47. *Report to the Primary School Committee on the Abolition of the*

Schools for Colored Children with the City Solicitor's Opinion (Boston: J. H. Eastburn, 1846), p. 19. I am indebted to Ms. Marie Lamoureux of the American Antiquarian Society for bringing this uncataloged AAS document to my attention.

48. Horton and Horton, *In Hope of Liberty*, p. 217. For more on the Crandall story, see Samuel May, *The right of colored people to education, vindicated letters to Andrew T. Judson, Esq. and others in Canterbury, remonstrating with them on their unjust and unjustifiable procedure relative to Miss Crandall and her school for colored females* (Brooklyn, Conn.: Advertiser Press, 1833); Philip Foner and Josephine Pacheco, eds., *Three Who Dared; Prudence Crandall, Margaret Douglass, Myrtilla Miner: Champions of Antebellum Black Education* (Westport, Conn.: Greenwood Press, 1984); Edmund Fuller, *Prudence Crandall: An Incident of Racism in Nineteenth-Century Connecticut* (Middletown: Wesleyan University Press, 1971); and Susan Strane, *A Whole-Souled Woman: Prudence Crandall and the Education of Black Women* (New York: W. W. Norton, 1990). The persecution of Margaret Douglass, a teacher imprisoned for teaching free southern children of color, is another important example of resistance to African American education. See *The personal narrative of Miss Margaret Douglass, A Southern woman, who was imprisoned for one month in the common jail of Norfolk, under the laws of Virginia, for the crime of teaching free colored children to read* (Boston: John P. Jewett, 1854).

49. Paul's endorsement of supportive learning environments for African American students was in keeping with the positions of African American leaders in other northern cities. See John Rury, "The New York African Free School, 1827–1836: Conflict over Community Control of Black Education,"

Phylon 44 (1983): 187–197; and Curry, *The Free Black in Urban America*, esp. chap. 10. In *The Education of Black Philadelphia: The Social and Educational History of a Minority Community, 1900–1950* (Philadelphia: University of Pennsylvania Press, 1979), Vincent Franklin discusses Philadelphia's segregated schools and the racial tensions that negatively influenced African American enrollments and promoted particular community platforms advocating all-black schools and the employment of black teachers in these schools. For histories of African American education, see Levesque, *Black Boston;* Carter Woodson, *The Education of the Negro Prior to 1861* (New York: G. P. Putnam, 1915); and Arna Bontemps and Jack Conroy, *They Seek a City* (Garden City, N.Y.: Doubleday, Doran, 1945).

50. These authenticating documents were usually authored by the narrative's amanuensis and editor, abolitionists, family friends, and even slaveholders. See Robert Stepto, *From behind the Veil: A Study of Afro-American Narrative* (Urbana: University of Illinois Press, 1979), on the slave narrative genre and the effect of authenticating materials. Other studies of the genre include Stephen Butterfield, *Black Autobiography in America* (Amherst: University of Massachusetts Press, 1974); Frances Smith Foster, *Witnessing Slavery: The Development of Antebellum Slave Narratives* (Madison: University of Wisconsin Press, 1979); Henry Louis Gates and Charles T. Davis, eds., *The Slave's Narrative* (Oxford: Oxford University Press, 1985); Ronald Judy, *(Dis)Forming the American Canon: African-Arabic Slave Narratives and the Vernacular* (Minneapolis: University of Minnesota Press, 1993); and Valerie Smith, *Self-Discovery and Authority in Afro-American Narrative* (Cambridge, Mass.: Harvard University Press, 1987).

51. Slave narrators were also highly conscious of their audiences. In *Witnessing Slavery,* Frances Foster describes the kind of readers that they anticipated and discusses the kinds of differences that probably existed between black writers and white readers. Susan Paul clearly envisioned a northern, multiracial readership with whom she shared beliefs about the centrality and redemptive power of spiritual education.

52. "The Little Blind Boy," inspired by alleged events at Boston's New England Institution for the Blind, was published in at least three northern periodicals before it appeared in the *Memoir:* the *Sabbath School Instructor,* June 18, 1834, p. 13; the *Anti-Slavery Record* 1 (1835): 11; and *The Liberator,* February 28, 1835, p. 36. The *Sabbath School Instructor,* an evangelical periodical for children, their parents, and their Sabbath school teachers, was published by the Maine Sabbath School Union in Portland. Issues listed James Loring, Paul's future publisher, as an individual authorized to receive subscription payments and forward them to the publishers.

   "Am I to Blame?" was also published in the *Sabbath School Instructor,* July 2, 1834, p. 123.

53. In the *Memoir* Paul states that "The Little Blind Boy" was written by "Some one who loves little children." In the *Sabbath School Instructor* the poet is identified by the initial "J." Garrison's reprinting of the piece in *The Liberator* spurred Samuel Howe, director of the New England Institution for the Blind, to write to the paper to refute the poet's charge of race prejudice. Howe's letter was published on July 18, 1835, just weeks after the first excerpts of Paul's *Memoir* appeared in the paper. Lydia Maria Child challenged Howe's assertions in a July 25, 1835, article, and the final spirited exchange between the two was published on August 1, 1835.

54. For a detailed discussion of American Sunday School Union pedagogical methods and manuals designed to promote intellectual and spiritual growth, see Anne Boylan's excellent study of antebellum evangelical education, *Sunday School: The Formation of an American Institution, 1790–1880* (New Haven: Yale University Press, 1988), chap. 5.

55. Anne Scott MacLeod, *A Moral Tale: Children's Fiction and American Culture, 1820–1860* (Hamden, Conn.: Shoe String Press, 1975), p. 21. According to MacLeod, just six years after its founding in 1824, the Philadelphia-based ASSU had issued approximately six million volumes of Sunday school material and had an annual budget of just over $75,000. For a detailed analysis of the ASSU's politics, distribution policies, and educational agendas, see Boylan, *Sunday School.*

56. Edwin Wilbur Rice, *The Sunday-School Movement, 1780–1917, and the American Sunday School Union, 1817–1917* (Philadelphia: American Sunday School Union, 1917), p. 68; Janet Cornelius, "'We Slipped and Learned to Read': Slave Accounts of the Literacy Process, 1830–1865," *Phylon* 44 (September 1983): 179.

57. In their discussions of the legal backlash against African Americans following the Nat Turner revolt, both Janet Cornelius and Wilma King state that although slave states did introduce laws limiting African Americans' access to education, the extensiveness of such prohibitions has been exaggerated. See Cornelius, "'We Slipped and Learned to Read'"; and Wilma King's groundbreaking study of slave children, *Stolen Childhood* (Bloomington: University of Indiana Press, 1995), esp. chap. 4.

58. William S. McFeely, *Frederick Douglass* (New York: W. W. Norton, 1991), p. 43. There is some disagreement about

whether Douglass was indeed conducting a Sabbath school in which the gospel was being taught. McFeely asserts that Douglass was teaching the gospel to young black children in St. Michaels, Maryland, whereas King, *Stolen Childhood*, asserts that Douglass did not provide religious instruction and that the school simply met on the Sabbath.

59. Boylan, *Sunday School*, p. 82. The ASSU's response to slavery should be contextualized in relation to evangelical practices and outreach in the South. Although leading American denominations such as the Baptists, Methodists, and Presbyterians had a history of educating and converting slaves, in the late 1830s and early 1840s slavery and African American education—secular and religious—produced intense sectionalism and schism within the churches. For discussions of these crises, see the essays by Chris Padgett, Randy Sparks, Beth Barton Schweiger, Edward Crowther, and John McKivigan in John McKivigan and Mitchell Snay, eds., *Religion and the Antebellum Debate over Slavery* (Athens: University of Georgia Press, 1998).

60. For detailed discussions of the changes in formal Sabbath school education for African Americans during slavery and in the aftermath of the Nat Turner revolt, see Boylan, *Sunday School*, esp. chap. 3; King, *Stolen Childhood*, esp. chap. 4; John Quist, "Slaveholding Operatives of the Benevolent Empire: Bible, Tract, and Sunday School Societies in Antebellum Tuscaloosa County, Alabama," *Journal of Southern History* 42 (August 1996): 481–526; and Cornelius, "'We Slipped and Learned to Read.'"

61. At present there is neither a comprehensive history of the American Sabbath School Society in Boston nor a detailed ac-

count of African American Sabbath schools. Although this
lack of information makes it difficult to elaborate further on
the organization's publication policies and institutional racism,
it is clear that racial prejudice and conservative racial politics
informed the policies of the Sabbath school organization. On
July 9, 1831, *The Liberator* reported that at a Fourth of July
Sabbath school exhibition held at the Park Street Church, "the
colored boys were permitted to occupy pews one fourth of the
way up the side aisle." The editor continued wryly, "The next
stride, we trust, will carry them up to the pulpit. N. B. The colored girls took their seats near the door as usual." On the other
hand, some five years later Susan Paul's Sabbath school class
received an encouraging letter and donation from the white
children of the Union Evangelical Sabbath School of Amesbury and Salisbury, Massachusetts. The letter, published in
The Liberator on August 13, 1836, underscored the children's
awareness of slavery, racism, and inequality and ended with an
earnest wish for universal liberty and happiness. For this letter
and Paul's response, see pages 123–127.

62. MacLeod, *A Moral Tale*, p. 22.
63. Similarly, Jarena Lee, author of *The Life and Religious Experi-
    ence of Jarena Lee, a Coloured Lady* (1836), faced considerable
    opposition from the African American religious press in 1842
    when she submitted a revised edition for republication. See
    William Andrews, *Sisters of the Spirit: Three Black Women's
    Autobiographies of the Nineteenth Century* (Bloomington: Indi-
    ana University Press, 1986); and Frances Foster, *Written by
    Herself: Literary Production by African American Women, 1746–
    1892* (Bloomington: Indiana University Press, 1993), for a dis-
    cussion of Lee's experiences and the constraints—racial, so-

cial, and political—placed upon nineteenth-century African
American women writers. Harriet Wilson, author of *Our Nig*
(1859), also suffered as a result of negligible institutional and
community support. For a discussion of her plight, see the in-
troduction by Henry Louis Gates Jr. in the 1987 edition of the
text.

64. *The Liberator,* August 1, 1835, p. 122. The writer identified
himself or herself only as "One Whose Heart Has Been
Warmed with the Simple Story of Little James."

65. James Loring (1770–1850) was involved in bookselling and
publishing for most of his life. He began his printing career
with William Manning, who became his long-term business
partner. Loring was the publisher of the *Massachusetts Register*
for nearly fifty years (1801–1847) and editor of the *Christian
Watchman* from 1826 through 1834. He was also the treasurer
of the Boston Baptist Foreign Missionary Society. Boston city
directories reveal that until the early 1820s Loring's press and
bookshop were located at Number 2 Cornhill, in the heart of
Boston's publishing district and close to antislavery publishers
and organizations. He published and distributed Paul's manuscript from his next place of business, at 132 Washington
Street, in the city's new hub of printing activity.

66. Some of the representative texts Loring published in the years
preceding the publication of the *Memoir of James Jackson* included *The young Jewess: a narrative; illustrative of the Polish
and English Jews of the present century, exhibiting the superior
moral influence of Christianity* (1827) and an 1830 reprint of
Experience Mayhew's 1727 *Narratives of the lives of pious Indian women: who lived on Martha's Vineyard more than one hundred years since.*

67. Rebecca Warren Brown, *Memoir of Mrs. Chloe Spear: a native of Africa, who was enslaved in childhood, and died in Boston, January 3, 1815, aged 65 years* (Boston: James Loring, 1832), p. 90. Warren mentions that the Reverend Thomas Paul attended Mrs. Spear's funeral. Spear was not one of Paul's parishioners; in 1788 she had become a member of the Second Baptist Church.

68. The Anti-Slavery Society Bookshop was still actively promoting the *Memoir of James Jackson* in 1837, and *The Liberator* consistently included it in its page-long advertisements. The *Memoir* was priced at twenty-five cents, the cost of a ticket to a Juvenile Choir concert.

69. The Oberlin College copy has the Massachusetts Anti-Slavery Society's acronym penciled on its flyleaf. The Oberlin Collegiate Library Collection, which was started in 1833, when the school was a religious institute, received library donations from ministers around the country.

70. The acquisition records of the Brothers in Unity show that *The Memoir* was donated to the society library with two other volumes frequently advertised by the Massachusetts Anti-Slavery Society: the *Memoir of Wilberforce* and *The Memoir of Phillis Wheatley*. The copy of the *Memoir of James Jackson* originally donated to Yale is now held by Columbia University, and there is no conclusive documentation to explain how the volume was transferred from one institution to the other. Below the Yale University bookplate is the signature "B. Wright." Neither the identity nor school affiliation of this individual has yet been determined. This discovery also means that there may be only five, rather than six, extant copies of the *Memoir*. The other copies are located at the American Anti-

quarian Society, the General Theological Seminary of the Protestant Episcopal Church, Oberlin College, and The Library Company of Philadelphia.

71. Edward B. Coe, "The Literary Societies," in *Yale College: A Sketch of Its History,* ed. William L. Kingsley (New York: Henry Holt, 1879), pp. 307–323; quotation p. 308.

72. Foster, *Written by Herself,* p. 46.

73. Anne Scott MacLeod, *American Childhood: Essays on Children's Literature of the Nineteenth and Twentieth Centuries* (Athens: University of Georgia Press, 1994), pp. 136, 137.

74. Patricia Demers, *Heaven upon Earth: The Form of Moral and Religious Children's Literature, to 1850* (Knoxville: University of Tennessee Press, 1993), p. 21.

75. Child's periodical was published too late for Paul to have read it as a girl, but as a teacher she probably read selections to her students. For an informative account of Child's works for juveniles, see Carolyn Karcher, *First Woman of the Republic: Lydia Maria Child* (Durham, N.C.: Duke University Press, 1994). It is also possible that Paul, who enjoyed close professional ties to Child during this time, contributed to Child's periodical, in which the authors of items remained anonymous.

76. On nineteenth-century reader response to evangelical narratives, see Gillian Avery, "Children's Books and Social History," in *Research about Nineteenth-Century Children and Books,* ed. Selma Richardson (Urbana-Champaign: University of Illinois Press, 1980), pp. 23–41.

77. Ibid., p. 30.

78. "A Word or Two to Teachers," *Sabbath School Instructor,* June 22, 1831, p. 15. The insistence on death in evangelical literature was of course influenced by the high mortality rates for infants

and children. Jacqueline Reinier notes that in the 1820s, for instance, children under the age of ten accounted for more than 40 percent of all deaths in the United States; *From Virtue to Character: American Childhood, 1775–1850* (New York: Twayne, 1996). Other scholars suggest that in the antebellum period most children under the age of ten had experienced the death of a family member. For additional discussions of death and nineteenth-century childhood, see Peter Gregg Slater, *Children in the New England Mind in Death and in Life: From the Puritans to Bushnell* (Hamden, Conn.: Archon Books, 1977); and David Stannard, *The Puritan Way of Death: A Study in Religion, Culture, and Social Change* (New York: Oxford University Press, 1977).

79. *The Liberator* reprinted numerous anecdotal accounts of good children, but the characters were rarely assigned racial characteristics. Short stories such as Lydia Maria Child's "Mary French and Susan Easton," in which an African American child is abducted and sold into slavery while her white friend is rescued and restored to her family, were typical of the contexts in which African American children appeared. Paul's documentary history and narrative exceed the usual limits of contemporary juvenile fiction or journalistic anecdotes.

80. The emphasis on death as a vehicle for family reunion pervaded evangelical periodicals for children. In a July 1837 issue of the Boston-based *Sabbath School Messenger*, for instance, the discussion between two young girls about death involves a series of questions and heartfelt answers about their fathers' passing, the men's roles in heaven, and the opportunities for reunion that await obedient Christian daughters and sons. This article, titled "A Dialogue on Death," was, according to the

editorial note, originally presented at the Sabbath School Anniversary in Portland, Maine, and reprinted in the *Maine Wesleyan Journal.*

81. On antebellum African American education and literacy as well as resistance to African American intellectual advancement, see Thomas Webber, *Deep like the Rivers: Education in the Slave Quarter Community, 1831–1865* (New York: W. W. Norton, 1978); Foner and Pacheco, *Three Who Dared;* and Janet Cornelius, *When I Can Read My Title Clear: Literacy, Slavery, and Religion in the Antebellum South* (Columbia: University of South Carolina Press, 1963). On postbellum African American education, see James Anderson, *The Education of Blacks in the South, 1860–1935* (Chapel Hill: University of North Carolina Press, 1988); Vincent Franklin, *The Education of Black Philadelphia: The Social and Educational History of a Minority Community, 1900–1950* (Philadelphia: University of Pennsylvania Press, 1979); Audrey McCluskey, "'We Specialize in the Wholly Impossible': Black Women School Founders and Their Mission," *Signs* 22 (Winter 1997): 403–426; and Robert Morris, *Reading, 'Riting, and Reconstruction: The Education of Freedmen in the South, 1861–1870* (Chicago: University of Chicago Press, 1981). Carter G. Woodson, *The Education of the Negro prior to 1861: A History of the Education of the Colored People of the United States from the Beginning of Slavery to the Civil War* (Washington, D.C.: Association for the Study of Negro Life and History, 1919), pp. 170–171; also quoted in Webber, *Deep like the Rivers,* p. 29. Nineteenth-century African American texts on African American reading practices, strategies for learning, and educational opportunities include Olaudah Equiano, *The Interesting Narrative of the Life*

of Olaudah Equiano or Gustavus Vassa, the African (1814);
Frederick Douglass, *Narrative of the Life* (1845); Harriet Wilson, *Our Nig* (1859); and Charlotte Forten's mid-nineteenth-century diaries.

82. King, *Stolen Childhood,* p. 74.

83. According to Anne Boylan, Sabbath school pedagogy was based on catechism and question books. Although there are no records of the materials Susan Paul and other instructors used in the African American Sabbath schools, the *Memoir* confirms that Susan Paul employed these standard Sabbath School pedagogical methods in her classroom.

84. Holly Keller reviews the problematics and social politics that inhibited schoolroom discussions of slavery in antebellum American classrooms. She argues that selected books "frequently oversimplified important issues like slavery in order to avoid the dilemma posed by the more obvious moral inconsistencies." Keller asserts that "Northern schoolbooks expressed passion on such subjects as religion, patriotism, and honesty, but not about abolition" and that "even an educational reformer like Horace Mann, who certainly made the connection between moral education and social reform, skirted the issue of abolitionism in the schools"; "Juvenile Antislavery Narrative and Notions of Childhood," *Children's Literature* 24 (1996): 86–100; quotations p. 93. Carolyn Karcher's discussion of the boycott of Lydia Maria Child's *Juvenile Miscellany* and Child's inability to maintain sales of the previously popular children's magazine after introducing racial matters shows that poor sales also deterred publishers from printing such materials. For a discussion of Child's juvenile literature and publication woes, see Karcher, *First Woman of the Republic.*

85. Boylan, *Sunday School*, p. 40.
86. This comment refers only to biblical writing in the interval between the Old and New Testaments.
87. Keller, "Juvenile Antislavery Narrative," p. 87.
88. Paul's text, with its emphasis on literacy and education as evidence of a child's freedom, stands in compelling contrast to Frederick Douglass' *Narrative of the Life*, in which he notes that as a child, his realization of his enslavement stemmed in part from the realization that he was ineligible for education— secular or spiritual.
89. The first American Sabbath schools were organized in 1791. These schools, which met on Sundays, were meant to instruct children and adults in Bible learning as well as in basic reading and writing. A number of children who were unable to attend regular primary or private schools during the week received their only exposure to formal education through the Sabbath schools. In the 1820s and 1830s there were at least three officially recognized African American Sabbath schools on Southac and Belknap Streets, catering to children and adults. The Southac Street school had seven teachers, and most of the fifty students were African American. There were two Belknap Street African Sabbath schools, one for young children and the other for adults. See the *First Annual Report of the Massachusetts Sabbath School Union, Presented at the First Annual Meeting, June 1, 1826* (Boston: T. R. Marvin, 1826), pp. 10–12, 27.
90. *The Liberator*, August 13, 1836, p. 130.
91. In 1830 approximately two million of the 2,328,642 African Americans in the United States were slaves.
92. Gillian Avery and Angela Bull, *Nineteenth Century Children: Heroes and Heroines in English Children's Stories, 1780–1900* (London: Hodder and Stoughton, 1965), p. 220.

93. Ibid., p. 223.
94. Ibid., p. 225.
95. For more on nineteenth-century consolation literature, see Anne Douglas, "Heaven Our Home: Consolation Literature in the Northern United States, 1830–1860," in *Death in America*, ed. David Stannard (Philadelphia: University of Pennsylvania Press, 1975), pp. 49–68; and Slater, *Children in the New England Mind in Death and in Life*.
96. Jay Holbrook, *Massachusetts Vital Records, Boston 1630–1849: Death and Burials, 1833–1836*, vol. 26 (Oxford, Mass.: Holbrook Research Institute, 1985).
97. MacLeod, *American Childhood*, p. 137.
98. Ibid., p. 122.

MEMOIR

1. The source of this quotation has not yet been identified. Like other quotations in the *Memoir*, these lines may be from a nineteenth-century Sabbath school tract.
2. "The eyes of the Lord are in every place, beholding the evil and the good"; Proverbs 15:3.
3. The Creation story, Genesis 1:1–2:25.
4. The story of Noah and the Flood, Genesis 6:1–9:19.
5. "And it came to pass, when Moses had made an end of writing the words of this law in a book, until they were finished, That Moses commanded the Levites, which bare the ark of the covenant of the Lord, saying, Take this book of the law, and put it in the side of the ark of the covenant of the Lord your God, that it may be there for a witness against thee"; Deuteronomy 31:24–26.

6. The New Testament gospels of Matthew, Mark, Luke, and John.

7. "Therefore all things whatsoever ye would that men should do to you, do ye even so unto them: for this is the law and the prophets"; Matthew 7:12. The incident related here is reminiscent of an anonymous article titled "The Colored Boy," originally published in the *Sabbath School Instructor* and reprinted in the January 28, 1832, issue of *The Liberator*.

8. "And [Hagar] called the name of the Lord that spake unto her, Thou God seest me: for she said, Have I also here looked after him that seeth me?"; Genesis 16:13.

9. Isaac Watts, "When I can read my title clear," in *Hymns for Sunday School Teachers* (Philadelphia: I. Ashmead, 1826), p. 31.

10. "In my Father's house are many mansions: if it were not so, I would have told you. I go to prepare a place for you"; John 14:2.

11. The reference is to a specific line in the Lord's Prayer: "For if ye forgive men their trespasses, your Heavenly Father will also forgive you: But if ye forgive not men their trespasses, neither will your Father forgive your trespasses"; Matthew 6:14–15.

12. "Then said Jesus, Father, forgive them; for they know not what they do"; Luke 23:34.

13. The reference is to the life and death of the apostle Stephen, Acts 6–7.

14. "For when we were yet without strength, in due time Christ died for the ungodly"; Romans 5:6. "For I delivered unto you first of all that which I also received, how that Christ died for our sins according to the Scriptures"; 1 Corinthians 15:6. "For God hath not appointed us to wrath, but to obtain salvation by our Lord Jesus Christ, Who died for us, that, whether we wake

or sleep, we should live together with him"; 1 Thessalonians
5:9–10.

15. "Ye have heard that it hath been said, Thou shalt love thy
neighbor, and hate thine enemy"; Matthew 5:43.

16. Massachusetts Sunday School Union reports that might contain
information about this school have not been located and may
not be extant.

17. "And lead us not into temptation, but deliver us from evil: For
thine is the kingdom, and the power, and the glory, for ever.
Amen"; Matthew 6:13.

18. The Ten Commandments; Exodus 20:1–17.

19. "Remember the sabbath day, to keep it holy. Six days shalt
thou labor, and do all thy work: But the seventh day is the sabbath of the Lord thy God: in it thou shalt not do any work,
thou, nor thy son, nor thy daughter, thy manservant, nor thy
maidservant, nor thy cattle, nor thy stranger that is within thy
gates: For in six days the Lord made heaven and earth, the sea,
and all that in them is, and rested the seventh day: wherefore
the Lord blessed the sabbath day, and hallowed it"; Exodus
20:8–11 and 31:13–17.

20. "And he gave unto Moses, when he had made an end of com-
muning with him upon mount Sinai, two tables of testimony,
tables of stone, written with the finger of God"; Exodus 31:18.

21. "And it came to pass, when Moses had made an end of writing
the words of this law in a book, until they were finished, That
Moses commanded the Levites, which bare the ark of the covenant of the Lord, saying, Take this book of the law, and put it
in the side of the ark of the covenant of the Lord your God,
that it may be there for a witness against thee"; Deuteronomy
31:24–26.

22. Accounts of Christ meeting with his apostles, teaching in the synagogues, and healing the sick appear throughout the gospels, e.g., Matthew 12:1–15, Mark 3:1–6, Luke 13:10–17, and Luke 14:1–6.

23. The fourth commandment: "Remember the sabbath day, to keep it holy"; Exodus 20:8; "Keep the sabbath day to sanctify it, as the Lord thy God hath commanded thee"; Deuteronomy 5:12.

24. "I must not sin as many do," in *The Sunday-School Child's Hymn Book* (Philadelphia: American Sunday School Union [1848–1853]), p. 11, lines 7–8.

25. James's exclamation appears to be based on Revelation 19:1: "And after these things I heard a great voice of much people in heaven, saying, 'Alleluia; Salvation, and glory, and honor, and power, unto the Lord our God.'"

26. The hymn that James begins to sing here may be based on "Suffer little children to come unto me," a recitative and chorus that Susan Paul's Juvenile Choir performed often in the 1830s. The song's lyrics, based on Matthew 19:13–15, are printed in one of the few extant Juvenile Concert programs: "And they brought unto Jesus, young children, that he should touch them: and his disciples rebuked those that brought them. But when Jesus saw it, he was much displeased, and said unto them:—Suffer little children to come unto me, and forbid them not, for of such is the kingdom of heaven. Hallelujah—Praise ye the Lord—Hallelujah—Amen"; Juvenile Concert program, February 9, 1837, Samuel J. May Anti-Slavery Collection, Cornell University.

27. The Reverend Samuel Snowden was pastor of the May Street African Methodist Episcopal Church on Beacon Hill from 1826 until his death in 1850. Snowden was an outspoken civil rights

and abolitionist activist whom William Lloyd Garrison once referred to as the "Thomas Paul of our day" (George Levesque, *Black Boston: African American Life and Culture in Urban America, 1750–1860* [New York: Garland, 1994], p. 290). David Walker, author of the incendiary *Walker's Appeal . . . to the Coloured Citizens of the World*, was one of Snowden's parishioners and a close friend. Snowden's presence at James's deathbed suggests that the Jackson family may have attended his church or that James attended the May Street Sabbath school. Snowden was one of the few African American Sabbath school superintendents in Boston. In 1826 the African Methodist school under his supervision had five male teachers, seven female teachers, and sixty students; *First Annual Report of the Massachusetts Sabbath School Union*, p. 27. Attendance records for this school have yet to be located, so it is not possible to confirm whether James Jackson attended this Sabbath school.

28. "Then there were brought unto him little children, that he should put his hands on them, and pray: and the disciples rebuked them. But Jesus said, Suffer little children, and forbid them not, to come unto me; for of such is the kingdom of heaven. And he laid his hands on them, and departed thence"; Matthew 19:13–15.

29. Ibid.

30. "In my Father's house are many mansions; if it were not so, I would have told you. I go to prepare a place for you"; John 14:2.

31. Matthew 19:15.

32. These three instructions are based on Genesis 16:13, Matthew 5:44, and Matthew 7:12, respectively.

33. Isaac Watts, "Come, let us join our cheerful songs," in *The Re-*

vivalist: A Collection of Choice Revival Hymns and Tunes, ed. Joseph Hillman (Rochester, N.Y.: Hillman, 1869), p. 35.

34. Although Paul does not identify any specific institution, at this time the New England Institution for the Education of the Blind was located at 19 Pearl Street in Boston. Its president was Jonathan Phillips, and its trustees included Samuel May and Horace Mann.

35. "And hath made of one blood all nations of men for to dwell on all the face of the earth, and hath determined the times before appointed, and the bounds of their habitation"; Acts 17:26.

36. "Then Peter opened his mouth, and said, Of a truth I perceive that God is no respecter of persons"; Acts 10:34.

ARTICLES AND LETTERS

1. The Salem Anti-Slavery Society, organized on January 27, 1834, by July 1834 had 420 members, 11 of whom were local ministers. Susan Paul and all the Boston speakers were members of the New England Anti-Slavery Society.

Professor Charles Follen (1796–1840) of Milton, Massachusetts, was a Harvard professor of German literature. For additional biographical information, see *The Letters of William Lloyd Garrison,* vol. 1, ed. Walter Merrill (Cambridge, Mass.: Harvard University Press, 1971). For accounts of his participation in the abolitionist struggle and his role in the New England Anti-Slavery Society, see *Annual Reports of the Massachusetts Anti-Slavery Society,* vols. 1–10: *1833–1842* (Westport, Conn.: Negro Universities Press, 1970).

Reverend E. M. P. Wells (1793–1878) was an Episcopal minister, vice president of the Massachusetts Anti-Slavery Society, and an active abolitionist speaker. In 1836 Wells was the rector of a Boston "school for moral discipline" at South Boston Point; *Stimpson's Boston Directory* (Boston: Charles Stimpson Jr., 1836), p. 372. For additional biographical information, see Merrill, *Letters of Garrison*, vol. 1.

Rev. Amos Augustus Phelps, a graduate of Yale Divinity School and the founder of the American Anti-Slavery Society, was the minister at Boston's Pine Street Trinitarian Church. By the late 1830s he was an agent for the Massachusetts Anti-Slavery Society. For additional biographical information, see Merrill, *Letters of Garrison*, vol. 1; and C. Peter Ripley, ed., *The Black Abolitionist Papers*, vol. 3: *The United States, 1830–1846* (Chapel Hill: University of North Carolina Press, 1991).

Samuel Sewall (1799–1888) was a Bostonian and cousin of the renowned abolitionist Samuel J. May. In 1834 this life member of the New England Anti-Slavery Society served as its corresponding secretary. For additional biographical information, see Merrill, *Letters of Garrison*, vol. 1.

2. In 1834 Reverend Henry Grew (1781–1862) was deeply committed to the New England abolitionist struggle. Shortly after the March meeting in Salem, he chaired the second annual New England Anti-Slavery Convention, held in Boston. For additional biographical information, see Merrill, *Letters of Garrison*, vol. 1. On his participation in the New England Anti-Slavery Society, see *Annual Reports of the Massachusetts Anti-Slavery Society*, vols. 1–10.

3. Reverend Cyrus P. Grosvenor, a Dartmouth College graduate, served as minister of the Second Baptist Church in Salem, Massachusetts, from October 1830 to November 1834. During

the 1830s he was also president of the Salem Anti-Slavery Society and an agent of the Essex County Anti-Slavery Society. Grosvenor worked alongside the poet John Greenleaf Whittier, who, after moving to Amesbury, Massachusetts, in 1836, served as the Essex society's corresponding secretary (*The Liberator,* January 14, 1837, p. 10). For more on Grosvenor's abolitionist activities, see *Annual Reports of the Massachusetts Anti-Slavery Society,* vols. 1–10.

4. The Remonds were one of Salem's most prominent African American families. Salem city directories for the early 1840s include listings for three Remonds living at 11 Pond Street: "Charles L.," "John, barber," and "John Jr., barber" (*Salem Directory and City Register* [Salem: Henry Whipple, 1842], p. 100). Two of John and Nancy Remond's eight children became influential abolitionists and lecturers. Charles Remond (1810–1873), the eldest son, joined the Massachusetts Anti-Slavery Society and in 1838 became its first African American lecturer. At the time of the Salem antislavery meeting attended by Paul and her choir, Charles Remond was the Salem agent for Garrison's *Liberator.* His sister Sarah Parker Remond (1826–1894) lectured with her brother in the United States and eventually went on an abolitionist speaking tour in England. After more than ten years as an abolitionist lecturer in Europe, she earned a medical degree from an Italian medical school and began practicing medicine in Florence, Italy. For more on the Remonds, see Pauline Hopkins, "Charles Lenox Remond," *Colored American Magazine,* May 1901, pp. 34–39; entries in Rayford Logan and Michael Winston, eds., *Dictionary of American Negro Biography* (New York: W. W. Norton, 1982);

and Darlene Clark Hine, Elsa Barkley Brown, and Rosalyn Terborg-Penn, *Black Women in America* (Brooklyn: Carlson, 1993).

5. The Union Evangelical Church, in Salisbury Point, Massachusetts, was dedicated on December 31, 1835. The first pastor was Reverend John Gunnison. See Joseph Merrill, *History of Amesbury Including the First Seventeen Years of Salisbury to the Separation in 1654; and Merrimac from Its Incorporation in 1876* (Haverhill: Franklin P. Stiles, 1880), p. 349; Emily B. Smith, *A Chronological Record of the Principal Events That Have Occurred in Amesbury, Massachusetts, from the Organization of the Township of Merrimac in 1638 to 1900* (Amesbury: J. E. Bierly, 1901), p. 21.

6. The second and third sentences of this paragraph evoke Paul's prose in the *Memoir*, especially James Jackson's prayer for the slaves and Paul's suggestion at the end of Chapter V that her readers "remember and offer the same prayer for slaves and all in distress." American Sabbath School Union reports seldom include itemized lists of the schools' libraries, but this correspondence suggests that these students had read the *Memoir* and been moved by its compelling discussion of slavery.

7. None of the 1830s records for the Massachusetts Sunday School Union mentions an A. Morrill.

8. The reference to Matthew 5:44 recalls Paul's use of this verse at the end of the *Memoir*.

9. The students were prepared to perform abolitionist and temperance songs often included in Paul's Juvenile Choir concerts.

10. References to African American temperance societies in Boston appear in *The Liberator*. In 1833 Susan Paul was a founding

member of an African American women's temperance society. Her involvement in this group may have resulted in the formation of a juvenile temperance society in the city.

11. Joshua Leavitt (1794–1873) was a prominent abolitionist, founder of the American Anti-Slavery Society, and editor of the American Sunday School Union newspaper, the *New York Evangelist*. For additional biographical information see Hugh Davis, *Joshua Leavitt: Evangelical Abolitionist* (Baton Rouge: Louisiana State University Press, 1990); and Louis Ruchames, ed., *The Letters of William Lloyd Garrison*, vol. 2 (Cambridge, Mass.: Harvard University Press, 1971).

12. The concert was held at the Artists' Gallery on Summer Street in downtown Boston. A copy of the concert program is included in the Samuel J. May Anti-Slavery Collection, Cornell University.

13. "I Am a Cuckoo," in *Songs of Yesterday: An Anthology of American Songs*, ed. Philip Jordan and Lillian Kessler (Garden City, N.Y.: Doubleday, Doran, 1941), pp. 280–281. Juvenile Choir advertisements and concert programs use the title "The Cuckoo."

14. This piece is not included in general bibliographies of American songs, in contemporary reference works that focus on antislavery songs, or in popular nineteenth-century antislavery song collections such as William Wells Brown's *The Anti-Slavery Harp* (Boston: Bela Marsh, 1848); John Collins, *The Antislavery picknick: a collection of speeches, poems, dialogues and songs; intended for use in schools and anti-slavery meetings* (Boston: H. W. Williams, 1842); and Jairus Lincoln's *Anti-slavery melodies, for the friends of freedom; prepared for the Hingham Anti-Slavery Society* (Hingham, Mass.: Elijah B. Gill, 1843).

See Vicki Eaklor, *American Antislavery Songs: A Collection and Analysis* (New York: Greenwood Press, 1988), for more information on nineteenth-century performance.

15. William Lloyd Garrison, "Ye who in bondage pine," in "Hymns for the *Liberator* Soiree, Friday Evening, January 24th, 1851," Broadside Collection, American Antiquarian Society, Worcester, Mass., reprinted in Eaklor, *American Antislavery Songs*, pp. 39–40. This hymn, sung to the tune of "America," was performed at the 1851 celebration of the newspaper's twenty years of publication. The Juvenile Choir's first documented performance of this song occurred on February 1, 1834, at Columbian Hall, Boston.

16. C. W. D., "Sons of Columbia! Awake!" *The Liberator*, October 26, 1833, p. 171. The Juvenile Choir first performed this piece at the February 1, 1834, Columbian Hall concert. See *The Liberator*, February 1, 1834, p. 19.

17. W. J. Snelling, "The Colored Man's Opinion of Colonization," in Collins, *The Anti-Slavery picknick*, p. 105; reprinted in Eaklor, American Antislavery Songs, p. 5. According to Eaklor, the song first appeared in the October 13, 1832, issue of *The Liberator*. The title used by the New England correspondent is taken from the song's refrain.